TATIANNA

Monica,
    Animals are our friends and animals are our teachers.
    Connect with them in the "present moment" and some of the mysteries of life will magically be revealed to you.
    Through God all things are possible.

Warm Purrs,
Linda A. Mohr
12-10-07

TATIANNA

Tales and Teachings of My Feline Friend

LINDA A. MOHR

iUniverse, Inc.
New York Lincoln Shanghai

TATIANNA
Tales and Teachings of My Feline Friend

iUniverse books may be ordered through booksellers or by contacting:

iUniverse
2021 Pine Lake Road, Suite 100
Lincoln, NE 68512
www.iuniverse.com
1-800-Authors (1-800-288-4677)

Because of the dynamic nature of the Internet, any Web addresses or links contained in this book may have changed since publication and may no longer be valid.

ISBN: 978-0-595-42677-5 (pbk)
ISBN: 978-0-595-68130-3 (cloth)
ISBN: 978-0-595-87007-3 (ebk)

Printed in the United States of America

In loving memory of Tatianna

Tatianna's
Circle of Life Gallery

Captivation
Tatianna

CONTENTS

ACKNOWLEDGMENTS

I wish to express heartfelt gratitude to

- my great creator, God, for blessing me with life and love;

- my inspirational mother, Rosemary Barr Mohr, for instilling in me a passion for learning and words;

- my beloved felines, Tatianna, Noelle, Taittinger, Marnie, and Katarina, for gracing my life and inspiring this book;

- my compassionate veterinarians, Dr. Hope Wright and Dr. Pam Wood, for providing Tatianna's loving and devoted care;

- my soul mate, Charles Kenneth Kraft, for spiritually guiding me from the light side of the world to bring this message to the readers;

- my visionary life coach, Sacha, for enlightening me and illuminating my way along this incredible journey;

- my enthusiastic manuscript readers, Donna Link, Davee LaBay, and Dr. Alan Herron, for encouraging me with their helpful remarks and sincere interest;

- my creative editor, Anna Trusky, for guiding me clearly and confidently through the revisions and the Web site copywriting;

- my talented graphics artist, Deb Prater, for creating Tatianna's Circle of Life Gallery and Tatianna's Timeline from my amateur photographs;

- my respected colleague and computer expert, Dawn Musgrave-Demarest, for formatting and fine-tuning the manuscript;

- my incredible cat portrait artist, Drew Strouble, for capturing the essence of Tatianna's spirit through her light-spilling blue eyes;

- my foreword author and special friend, Rita M. Reynolds, for understanding, supporting, and promoting Tatianna's message of the miraculous power of love;

- my dear friend, Nikki Sweet, for sharing her insight on our spiritual connection to animals, for connecting me with Sacha, and for designing the book's Web site;

- my loving companion and confidant, Joseph Schilli, for enriching my life beyond words.

To each and every one of you, I could have not completed this project without your support and contributions. May God richly bless you.

FOREWORD

I sit on the floor next to my cat Lucy's cushion and watch her sleep. I must be smiling, but tears now pour down my face as joy and sorrow—inseparably mixed—ride through me like the incoming tide, for I know two absolute certainties: Lucy is very old and in failing health (she will not be with me in physical form much longer), and she is still so very beautiful. I sit here honored to know her and care for her these eighteen years and awed by the way she radiates grace and peace, despite being blind and deaf and in chronic renal failure.

There is another reason for the intensity of my feelings, and that is what has immediately drawn me up the spiral stairs to the loft where Lucy takes her naps. I have just finished reading the manuscript for *Tatianna—Tales and Teachings of My Feline Friend*, and I am compelled, right now, to tell all of the animals in my family how much I love and appreciate them. And so I have begun with Lucy.

Responsibility for an animal in one's care is all encompassing. It includes tending to not just their physical needs, but their emotional and, yes, spiritual needs as well—not in a religious sense, of course, but by being aware of their innate essence, which will continue beyond the end of their physical lives. It's not unlike raising a child, really, except for the sad fact (for us, their companions) that in all too short a time, these animals will begin to move into their elder years and then leave us to grieve for their absences. In those last years together, the relationship between human and animal changes dramatically, with the bond becoming increasingly intense—especially at the physical caregiving level. And it is a hard, painful labor. But here's the treasure: If we who care for these incredible beings can stay present and attuned to not only what they need, but what they teach us, we will be greatly enriched, our souls will deepen, and we will know that we have been left with a miraculous gift that can never leave us.

Linda Mohr offers, in the book you now hold in your hands, a magnificent view of the treasures given to her by Tatianna. But writing about her journey with her beloved cats, especially Tatianna, was no easy task. Linda is a courageous woman with an extraordinary sense of responsibility and commitment to those who share her home. By sharing Tatianna's story, she offers all of us a map by which we can ride high on the joyous times of such a relationship with our animal companions and, more importantly, navigate the tough, gut-wrenching, no-light-to-be-found times that will inevitably arise.

From the opening sentence to the last page of this special volume, Linda's devotion to, and acknowledgment of, the value of all life shines clearly—page after page, line after line. Her acceptance of workings greater than any of us can comprehend reminded me of the many times animals came to me in the most extraordinary circumstances, weaving magic through our shared lives and giving me equal—if not more—support and courage than I could ever give to them. My "angels," as I have always called them, arrived just when most needed, strong and centered when my own life was in frequent chaos. Certainly Linda, too, is more familiar with surviving tragedy than she would care to be. I wept for her losses and laughed with delight as her loving four-footed companions helped her cross those rocky passages.

I would venture to say that Tatianna was an "angel" for Linda, as were her other cats who lived before, during, and after Tatianna: Noelle, Taittinger, Marnie, and Katarina. From her writing, it is clear that Linda knows, in her soul, just how deep those relationships go and remain forever on levels we cannot explain.

I am so grateful to her for sharing her journey with Tatianna, offering insight and guidance into living with and caring completely for a cat in critical health, and the truth about her own painful emotional struggle with it all. In her tenderness toward her feline companions and her patience with the often unruly twists and turns of life, Linda reminds us that it is, overall, good to be alive and to trust the ones who walk through life with us, be they human or (if we are fortunate) animal. Thus, in Linda, I find a true friend and validation for all I believe in. I am confident that in reading this volume, you will feel the same.

Rita M. Reynolds, author of *Blessing The Bridge: What Animals Teach Us About Death, Dying, and Beyond*

PREFACE

Beginnings and endings are so similar.
Each is the start of an unknown journey, yet both
are equally important and are journeys
we have no choice but to take.[1]
—Nancy Dufresne

Growing up on a Midwestern Missouri farm, I was surrounded by a menagerie of animals, including barn cats, dogs, cows, chickens, rabbits, and pigs. Although the dogs and cats lived outdoors, I developed meaningful and unforgettable bonds with them. My dog's name was Penney, and her parents, Lady Bug and Brownie, were responsible for many litters of puppies on our farm over the years. My mother placed advertisements for free puppies in local newspapers. As a child, I always hoped no one would respond, but the puppies inevitably found new homes. It was always a sad moment when a puppy left, and I remember crying in my bedroom many a night.

My love of critters also included a pet turtle purchased at a Woolworth's store in Keokuk, Iowa. When I was seven years old, I had a turtle named Flaggie. He came with an American flag painted on the shell. He lived in a green ceramic bowl, which held a big rock. I still remember very poignantly being upset when Flaggie went missing one afternoon. When my mother went to the hospital to deliver my brother, she left Flaggie and me to spend a few days with Grandma and Grandpa Mohr. One morning, I looked in Flaggie's bowl, and he was not there. The bowl sat on the kitchen counter. I began wailing, and my grandmother came running into the kitchen to see what had happened to me. We began an all-out search. The countertop housed the usual kitchen gadgets, including a toaster, an electric skillet, a radio, and some canisters. Each item was pushed and pulled away from the back of the counter to see where Flaggie could have been. He was nowhere to be seen. Next, we started crawling around on the floor. I noticed it was a long way to the floor from the high countertops, and I could not imagine Flaggie falling that far down without injury. We searched the entire floor and still had no luck. Although I had calmed down to some degree while I was focused on the hunt, I quickly became hysterical when I realized that he was not in the kitchen. My grandmother kept repeating that he had to be somewhere in the kitchen. She began looking again on the countertop. This time, she picked up each gadget. When she picked up the toaster, guess who was there? I let out a squeal of relief and delight. Apparently, Flaggie had been under the toaster all along, and he had moved along with it during the first part of the search.

During my last summer at the University of Missouri, a stray Siamese cat adopted my roommate and me. We had moved to an apartment for three months. I suspected the former tenants had abandoned the cat. We began feeding the animal, and before we knew it, the cat was living in the house and sleeping with us. This was my first experience living with an indoor animal. I became fascinated with the cat and could not wait until the day I could have my own companion. At the end of the summer, I left for graduate school at Purdue University. My roommate remained behind to go to medical school, and the cat stayed with her. It was not until three years later, in 1975, that I got a cat.

In fact, my love of pets has led me to own, over a thirty-year period, five felines, including Noelle, Tatianna, Taittinger, Marnie, and Katarina. You will meet all of these adorable creatures throughout this book. I will share all that I have learned in living with them, loving them, and telling them good-bye. My love of pets also led me to be a partner in a one-stop pet care shop for thirteen years. This business included veterinarian, grooming, and boarding services and selling pet supplies. I have assisted in hundreds of surgeries, held the hands of grieving pet owners, and gained valuable insight into the physical and psychological behavior of animals. I have witnessed how an owner's love and devotion can help an animal overcome insurmountable medical odds.

When Tatianna entered my life as a kitten in 1985, I frankly did not ponder why this cat with a tremendous presence was with me. I did not question why we were beginning on this journey or what kind of ride it would be. Likewise, I did not contemplate what mysteries would be revealed to me during our common sojourn together. What I *did* know was that I simply adored the feline species as companions, and Tatianna was no exception. Unbeknownst to me, an invisible hand meticulously orchestrated this new journey to ensure the next chapter of growth in my life. Tatianna finding her way to my home was not by happenstance. Her path of joyous living and undaunted bravery had long been set in motion. Tatianna proved to be the pivotal player, adding inexpressible delight to my being and fostering excruciating spiritual growth. However, it was not until many years later that I recognized this astonishing benediction.

After Tatianna's life ended, a compelling force prompted me intuitively to explore and understand our heartfelt bond. If nothing else, I needed to record the fifteen and one-half years of love, devotion, faith, bravery, tenacity, triumph, loss, sorrow, acceptance, and perseverance. Writing about Tatianna was a way to celebrate her life and our blessed and precious adventure. The result of the writing was a tangible vehicle to preserve the poignant memories, ensuring that they would not become clouded in time. Recording lighthearted and affectionate tales about Tatianna was a way to gain continued strength to push forward to my next unknown destination. During this time of discovery and understanding as I pulled the grief close to me, I found that my life, experienced through Tatianna, had been forever altered. It revealed to me new insights about the interconnectedness of God and all of his creatures. I wanted to share this revelation to illuminate the way for others traveling a similar course. I believe we are all students and teachers throughout our lives. Tatianna taught me volumes about life and myself. Now, it is my turn to give back.

Just like the beginning and ending of our journey, I have recalled moments of great joy and contentment coupled with pangs of gut-wrenching despair and sorrow. My emotions have contracted and expanded like a yo-yo. While writing and reminiscing, I have laughed and cried until tears were streaming down my face, blurring the words before my eyes. The writing has been fun and occasionally effortless, but at the same time, it has been heartbreaking and often grueling. Despite this roller coaster of emotions, the invisible hand of God and the furry paws of Tatianna have guided me to clearly recollect in meticulous detail this story. I was challenged with the thought, "Tattie is gone—now, what can I learn from this lifelong intertwining of events?" I had no choice but to pursue the stirring in my heart.

It is now time for you to meet Tatianna.

Tatianna's Timeline

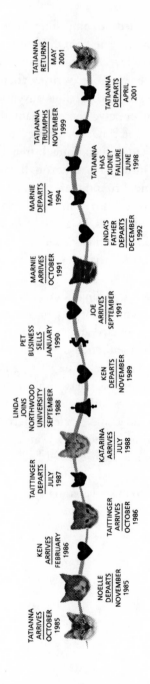

TATIANNA ARRIVES OCTOBER 1985

NOELLE DEPARTS NOVEMBER 1985

KEN ARRIVES FEBRUARY 1986

TAITTINGER ARRIVES OCTOBER 1986

TAITTINGER DEPARTS JULY 1987

KATARINA ARRIVES JULY 1988

LINDA JOINS NORTHWOOD UNIVERSITY SEPTEMBER 1988

KEN DEPARTS NOVEMBER 1989

PET BUSINESS SELLS JANUARY 1990

JOE ARRIVES SEPTEMBER 1991

MARNIE ARRIVES OCTOBER 1991

LINDA'S FATHER DEPARTS DECEMBER 1992

MARNIE DEPARTS MAY 1994

TATIANNA HAS KIDNEY FAILURE JUNE 1998

TATIANNA TRIUMPHS NOVEMBER 1999

TATIANNA DEPARTS APRIL 2001

TATIANNA RETURNS MAY 2001

PROLOGUE

**The spirit of faith shall heal the sick and
God shall raise him up.
The infinite healing presence is flowing
through Tatianna as harmony and health.
Tatianna is healed and whole.
She is joyful, eating and drinking, and enjoying life
with her loving companions, Katarina and Linda.
Tatianna is healed, blessed, and restored.
Through God, all things are possible.**
—Linda A. Mohr

I created this affirmation in June 1998 after my veterinarian, Dr. Hope Wright, told me how seriously ill Tatianna was. Tatianna was my beloved feline companion. Over the next thirty-four-month period, I softly and lovingly recited this affirmation while administering fluids to her daily. This ritualized affirmation, repeated more than two thousand times in that interval, became a healing and sustaining blessing for us both.

CHAPTER ONE
TATIANNA'S ARRIVAL

**We who choose to surround ourselves with
lives even more temporary than our own,
live within a fragile circle.**[1]
—Irving Townsend

In the fall of 1985, Tatianna fatefully found her way to me. She entered my circle of life when I was thirty-five years old. She remained there for fifteen and one-half years before it was her turn to exit. Throughout her time, Tatianna taught me that the purpose of life was to love unconditionally. She showed her unbounded love every day regardless of the circumstances. She showed me how to face life with courage. Even as a little kitten, when she needed to be brave, she never faltered.

However, I did not consciously go looking for her. In fact, adding a second cat to the household was the furthest thought from my mind. My life as a single woman was full with opening an antiques business, managing a pet business, earning an advanced degree, remodeling a 1950s home, and traveling abroad. Since 1977, I had partnered with my college sweetheart and opened the first one-stop shop for pet care in Palm Beach County in South Florida. The business offered medical, grooming, and boarding services as well as pet supplies. Although I owned the grooming and supply side—known as Pet Apothecary, I was integrally involved in all operations, especially during the start-up years. In addition to painting, remodeling, and cleaning the facility, I was a receptionist, bill collector, surgery and exam assistant, and groomer. I walked dogs, cleaned cages, and assisted in after-hour emergency care. I handled bank deposits, attended pet industry conventions, met with wholesalers, and selected merchandise. I consoled dying animals, assisted with euthanasia, and held the hands of grieving pet owners. The work was often demanding, and the hours were relentless, but the satisfaction of knowing I had helped to save or ease the suffering of an animal or simply provided preventive care was tremendously satisfying. Clients' animals became like family members. To lose one in any way, whether it was old age, cancer, or poisoning, always hurt.

Right before Tatianna arrived, I learned that my devoted cat, Noelle, had mouth cancer. Noelle was a beautiful orange marmalade cat with green, gleaming eyes; white boots; and a fluffy, white throat. She was a large cat, weighing in at fifteen pounds, with an immense presence. The minute I saw her, my long fascination with orange marmalade cats began. I named her Noelle, after my favorite Christmas carol, "The First Noel." Noelle filled my heart with countless hours of joy and contentment over the next ten years.

After Noelle was diagnosed with mouth cancer, I decided not to put her to sleep. Praying for a miraculous intervention, I had the tumor surgically removed. Although Noelle lived two months longer, I did not make the right decision for her quality of life. The regrettable choice haunted me. I vowed if ever given the chance again, I would do better. Little did I know that Tatianna would test that promise almost sixteen years later.

So in the midst of the traumatic letting go of Noelle, my business partner brought me an eight-week-old gray kitten from a client's litter. Of course, he thought this would help to ease my pain and heartache, but I felt vehemently otherwise at first. My concern was how Noelle would react to this sudden, unexpected, and most certainly unwelcome burst of life force now in the house. In retrospect, I was probably just as concerned about how I would emotionally handle a new kitten, because I was already depleted. Intuitively, I knew Noelle had entered the twilight of her life, so I wanted to ensure that absolutely nothing upset her unnecessarily. I thought a fractious, meowing, eight-week-old kitten that bounced off the furniture and teased Noelle unmercifully would lead to anything but a calm and peaceful ending.

Well, the gray kitten came, stayed, and prevailed. She was a Siamese and domestic short-hair mix with a dense grayish-blue coat that was set off by four white boots. Dark gray rings marked her front legs. Raccoon-like rings encircled her tail. Her throat and tummy were covered with soft white fur. A little pink nose and pink-lined ears accented her gray coloring. However, her wide, round, absorbing blue eyes were what really tugged at my heartstrings. Her mesmerizing eyes literally drew me into her soul with an immediate connection. They were purely and simply captivating. I could not help but wonder what mysteries were hidden beyond them. And she did not actually cause the havoc that I had expected. Even more surprising was that Noelle and I embraced her. It was years before I comprehended why this gray kitten arrived while Noelle was still living and I was saying farewell to her. But for all concerned—Noelle, the little gray kitten, and me—it could not have happened any other way.

I wanted an unusual and distinctive name for what was quite an unusual- and distinctive-looking kitten. I wanted a name that danced, a name that had a harmonious lilt to it. The name had to be different and sound pleasing and playful to the ear. Additionally, I wanted a name that could be shortened for fun. Russian names had always intrigued me. So the little gray kitten was named Tatianna. It fit her perfectly. Sometimes I called her "Tattie" or "Tat," and often I sang her names to her—"Tattie-Tatianna." This always made her eyes dance and her ears perk up, because she loved hearing those sounds strung together. And so did I. Her other pet names were "Sweetie-Tweetie" and "Boo," and she responded to all of them. But the majority of time I simply called her Tatianna.

Noelle passed away right after Thanksgiving in 1985. Although I had watched many animals die in the previous eight years of the pet business, and I had lost animals as a child, I was definitely not prepared for the inevitability of losing my precious feline companion of ten years. The hole in my heart was immense, as I had lost a piece of myself. It was Tatianna who got me through the darkness. Mornings without Noelle on my pillow, snuggled next to my face, would have seemed meaningless if it had not been for Tatianna. And without Noelle's welcoming presence, I would have dreaded returning home in the evenings if it had not been for Tatianna.

Tatianna was a bundle of lightheartedness from the minute I got up in the morning until I retired in the evening. A joyous aura of adventure surrounded her, and I could not help but smile just looking at her. Her companionship soothed me in my time of need. She was like an ointment of love, providing me with comfort and solace. Even as a kitten, she could intuit exactly what I needed to uplift my spirits. Sometimes, the trick was to play musical chairs with me. She watched me head for a particular chair, and she sprinted to it first and flopped down. Then, of course, I picked her up, lavished attention on her, and forgot momentarily about my pain. Or other times, she crawled up on my shoulder, hung her head down on my chest, and quietly fell asleep. Her gentle breathing calmed me down. Sometimes, her game was simply to meow loudly and dance around her food bowl.

I could almost hear her saying, "Hello! I'm here, and I'm hungry. What are you going to do about it, and how fast are you going to do it?"

That, at least, got me thinking about ceremoniously opening a can of food and putting it in Tatianna's bowl. Afterward, I thought about preparing my own meal.

Sometimes, she went off to hide and sleep. Although I quickly learned her favorite secret spots, there was one day when I could not find her, and I feared that she had slipped out the door when my housekeeper arrived. The two of us frantically looked for her for an hour. We continually called out her name and looked under beds, chairs, tables, and cushions. We opened drawers, closet doors, cabinets, and even the refrigerator. We simply could not find Tatianna.

I became as frightened as I had been when, as a little girl, my pet turtle was missing. Then I searched the living room for the fourth time. I just happened to walk up to the front picture window and slightly pull back a corner of the drapery. There, behind the drapery, was—guess who?—Tatianna. She was drowsing in the warm morning sunlight and was totally unaware of the chaos she had created. At any rate, she managed once again to get me to think about something besides my sorrow!

As much as Tatianna was able to help me mourn Noelle, she also needed consoling when Noelle died. Tatianna cried and cried the first day after Noelle's passing. Although they had only been together for a couple of months, Tatianna was clearly anguished and missing her new friend. That day, I realized just how much my little gray kitten needed me. So the first night, with just the two of us in the house, I cradled Tatianna in my arms, carried her up to my bedroom, and put her in bed with me. I think at that moment she understood how much I needed her and how much she needed me. Although she had a kitten bed in another room, she never again wanted to be alone at night. That started a lifelong routine of her sleeping with me.

We developed an extraordinary closeness in a short period of time, and that connection formed a foundation for us to help one another through the many twists and turns of our lives together. Our journey had begun!

Here I Come
Tatianna

Stately Stature
Noelle

Graceful on Pillow Top
Noelle

CHAPTER TWO
TATIANNA'S FIRST YEAR

The cat makes himself the companion of your hours of solitude, melancholy and toil. He remains for whole evenings on your knee, uttering his contented purr, happy to be with you and forsaking the company of animals of his own species. Put him down and he will jump up again, with a sort of a cooing sound that is like a gentle reproach; and sometimes he will sit upon the carpet in front of you, look at you with eyes so melting, so caressing, so human, that they almost frighten you; for it is impossible to believe that a soul is not there.[1]
—Theophile Gautier

Tatianna lived up to all of my expectations of a first-year kitty. She was mischievous, rambunctious, and curious. One minute, she was deliriously flying up and down the stairs, and the next moment, I found her collapsed and rolled up in a ball, napping.

My parents visited during Thanksgiving of 1985. To introduce herself, Tatianna chewed my father's shoelaces into pieces. He loved cats, so she picked the right houseguest's shoes! During Trivial Pursuit, she took great delight in being on the game board. I gently removed her from the fun and games and put her in the master bedroom, about twenty-five feet from where we were playing. She could still hear us talking and laughing and did not want to be left out. She cried and scratched at the closed door. After a few moments, my softhearted father went upstairs and brought her back down.

From then on, the only time I put her behind closed doors was for safety reasons, when a service person was working in the house or I had a large house party. In either situation, I did not want her to escape outside accidentally. She learned that I brought certain people into the closed room to ooh and aah over her, so she tolerated the temporary detention! From Trivial Pursuit forward, the household revolved around her, and she was included in all of the happenings if she wanted to be.

Tatianna's insatiable curiosity during her first year once led to a harrowing experience in the laundry room. I heard the washing machine shut off, and I went in the compact laundry room where there was barely room for a person, much less a washer and dryer. I transferred the clothes into the spin dryer, closed the door, and turned it on. A noise, which sounded like tennis shoes hitting the inside of the dryer, startled me. Because I knew I was drying lingerie, I immediately opened the door. To my astonishment, there was Tatianna in the dryer! She was stunned and shaken up, to say the least. Fortunately, only a couple of revolutions had been completed before I had stopped the machine.

I was so frightened by what could have happened. I thanked God for giving felines their nine lives! Tatianna undoubtedly used up her first one then. It was indeed a miraculous escape from a near-catastrophic accident. I had thought she was upstairs, but unbeknownst to me, Tatianna had followed me into the laundry room. While I was focused on transferring the wet clothes to the dryer, she had crawled into it. To this day, I always turn on the dryer for a few seconds, listen, stop it, and open the door to make sure no felines are inside. There have not been any more incidents in the laundry room!

Tatianna also loved shoes. As a kitten, she developed the habit of lying on the floor in front of my feet. She extended her paws and kneaded the top and toe of my shoes, rubbing them for several moments. This antic soon became Tatianna's distinctive trademark throughout her life. Whenever she saw me sit down, she came to me and performed this ceremonious ritual. I always had to be wearing shoes; however, it did not matter what kind or color. She kneaded tennis shoes, loafers, leather shoes, house slippers—you name it—as long as it was a shoe on my foot. She gazed up at me with her penetrating blue eyes, drawing me into her orb. And of course, her mesmerizing look and playful presence always elicited a loving response: a pat on the head, a soft-toned remark, a scratch behind the ears, or a lift up onto my lap.

During Tatianna's first year with me, a mutual friend introduced me to a man in February 1986 who would forever change my life. When we first met, we were both reeling from the dissolution of long-term relationships. Frankly, the last thing I wanted to do was go out on a date. Reluctantly, I met Ken for lunch at T.G.I. Friday's. It did not take me long to realize I was sitting across from one special guy. However, Tatianna did little to ingratiate herself with Ken during his first visit to my home. When he sat down on the couch, she ran over to greet him and bit his leg through his trousers. That antic took Ken quite by surprise. He did not know what to say except "Ouch!" At that moment, I wondered if I would ever see Ken again, and I am sure Ken wondered about my little gray hellion who was sharpening her teeth on his leg. But I did not have to worry for long. Tatianna always won her guests over with just a look, and Ken was no exception. Before I knew it, Tatianna was in his lap wanting attention. I could not wait for my turn to get Ken's attention as well. Ken had won me over with his deep, dark brown eyes. I felt that all of my questions about life were answered by his eyes.

Ken had movie-star looks. He resembled Burt Reynolds, walked like Tom Cruise, and talked like Dennis Weaver. He loved movies, and was cast as an extra a couple of times. We also went to a lot of shows. Our favorite movie was *Top Gun*, and our song was "Take My Breath Away." I could call him anytime of the day or night and hear that song playing in the background. Ken was also the funniest man I had ever met. He warmed my world with his never-ending repertoire of jokes and thoughtful phone calls. He always had a joke for the day that he shared with his coworkers at Pratt & Whitney. He called me numerous times over the course of the day. Sometimes, when I called his house, he answered the phone by saying, "Joe's Pool Hall, shoot!" I never knew from moment to moment what to expect from Ken. I loved his spontaneous approach to life. We enjoyed formally inviting each other to social events rather than calling each other, and so I never knew when I would receive a mailed invitation to a piano concert, Sunday brunch, or comedy routine.

We approached our relationship as if there were no tomorrows. Although our lives were already crammed with responsibilities before we met, we still found a way to live life to the fullest. Ken worked a lot of overtime, maintained his home, and raised his teenage children on his own. Ken also decided to return to college and was taking one or two night classes per term. We continuously acknowledged special little moments, gifts, and favors with as much fanfare as our trip to St. Maarten the first fall we were together. One of the things I adored about Ken was his knack for turning a routine day for me into an unforgettable day. One morning, when I checked out the weather outside, I noticed something under the windshield wipers of my car. I scurried downstairs and went out to investigate. A plastic bag protected an envelope with my name on it in Ken's handwriting. That marked the beginning of a long tradition of him swinging by my house on the way to work and leaving a card while I was still asleep. There was no set schedule, and that was part of the thrill for me. But it was always an exhilarating moment when I spotted the love letter on my car. It's a wonder I did not break a leg running through my trilevel home to get out there!

Ken was passionate about motorcycles and rode one to work most of the time. I had never grown up around motorcycles and frankly was afraid of them. One weekend, he took me for a ride. It was a once-in-a-lifetime experience. I was petrified the whole trip and never rode with him again, and he never pressured me to join him.

Ken never failed to ask about Tatianna when he called, and she never failed to greet him when he came to my home. She never repeated the biting incident, and they adored each other. I marveled at how Ken and Tatianna's approaches to living were similar. They were social, curious, and adventurous, and most of all, they loved unconditionally. Ken and I were each other's soul mates, lifelines, and best friends. He was unequivocally the man I wanted to spend the rest of my life with, and I could not wait to marry him. So 1985–86 was a momentous year for me—God had blessed my life with Tatianna and Ken, despite my reluctance of embracing a new kitten and a new man in my life. My breath was literally taken away each time I reconnected with Ken or looked into Tatianna's shimmering eyes. Life was good!

Kitty Kaper
Tatianna

CHAPTER THREE
TATIANNA'S NEW FRIEND,
TAITTINGER

Our perfect companions never have fewer than four feet.[1]
—Colette

During the fall of 1986, God blessed our lives for a mere moment with an orange marmalade kitten. I was jubilant to have found this incredibly special kitten. I named her Taittinger, after a French wine. Now Tatianna had a loving playmate with whom she could while away the days. She adored the new little kitten just like Noelle had adored Tatianna when she was a kitten. Tatianna clearly enjoyed the newfound companionship after being alone since Noelle's passing.

In July 1987, Taittinger suddenly became ill with an extremely high fever. She was diagnosed with feline infectious peritonitis. FIP, as it is commonly called, is a difficult viral disease to diagnose and to treat. Many veterinarians consider it to be the most common cause of unexplained fevers in cats. Lethargy, weight loss, eye disease, the swelling of the abdomen, and fluid in the chest can all occur with FIP. The disease usually occurs in cats under age two or over age thirteen. In Taittinger's case, she was less than a year old, and the high fever was her major symptom. She was going to pass on, but no one knew precisely how long we had left together.

I outfitted a tall cardboard box with soft towels for her and confined her in the downstairs guest bath and bedroom area away from Tatianna. Of course, Tatianna immediately intuited a change in the household happenings and continually tried to get into the closed-off rooms. I often sat with Tatianna and held her.

"Your little playmate is so very sick. It is just not safe for you to be around Taittinger and to sleep with her like you always have. I know you miss her terribly," I said, trying to console her.

During the last couple weeks of her life, I lovingly tended to Taittinger's every need at my home, where she was accustomed to being. She had to be fed and checked on every two hours, so during the night I repeatedly set the alarm and rose to care for her. I then fell back into bed until the next feeding. I was in a constant state of mental and physical exhaustion. Tatianna was not getting much sleep either. Sometimes, Ken convinced me to get a few extra hours of sleep, and he stayed at my house and cared for Taittinger through the darkest hours of the night. Tatianna settled in and snuggled in the crook of my legs. For a brief interlude, my love eased Tatianna's sadness over being separated from Taittinger. As I softly caressed her, I whispered words of reassurance to her.

"Tatianna, I will always take care of you, no matter what. I will always be there for you during our journey together."

On the last day of Taittinger's life, I held her at her midnight feeding. I lightly stroked her and talked softly to her. My heart was breaking for her. I could sense the end was nearing. Her breathing had changed to a raspy sound. I sat and held her for a long time. I was battling falling asleep, but I continued to hold Taittinger and rocked her in the chair. Around 1:30 AM, I placed her back in her box and intended to lay my head down for just a couple of moments. When the alarm woke me at 2:00 AM, the silence was deafening. There were no longer life sounds emanating from the box. I knew Taittinger was gone. I got up, turned on the light, and peeked into the box, knowing full well what I would see. I touched her; her little body was still warm. I was distraught that I was not awake by her side during her last breath. I prayed that Taittinger could sense how much I loved her and that I would always be with her in spirit. I prayed for the strength to take care of Tatianna. I was faced with having to tell her that Taittinger was gone. I called Ken, and he immediately came to my house. At 3:00 AM, he helped me place Taittinger in a black plastic bag. She was cremated the next day.

A few hours later, I destroyed Taittinger's bedding and cardboard box. I disinfected the downstairs area before opening it back up to Tatianna. Although I had told her that Taittinger was no longer with us, I knew she would explore every nook and cranny of the house, looking for her. And that she did—for days. She spent the first few hours in the downstairs bedroom, meowing loudly. She crawled under the bed, searching for her dear friend. Then she peeked under a table draped with a cloth. She wedged herself under the dresser and checked under the wingback chair. Then she wandered into the guest bath a few feet away and looked for Taittinger behind the shower curtain. I remained home with Tatianna the entire day. She simply would not leave the downstairs area. I moved her food and water bowls to the bedroom, but she was not interested in eating. After making all of her rounds, she started all over again by crawling under the bed. When she seemed convinced that Taittinger was not hiding under any of the furniture, she stationed herself on top of the bed, where she had a clear view of the outdoor entrance to the room as well as a view of another door that led to the bathroom and hall. She wanted to make sure she saw Taittinger when Taittinger returned. It was heartbreaking to watch, because I knew Taittinger would not be coming through either door.

The first evening after Taittinger's passing, I carried Tatianna up to the master suite. She had not slept all day, and I was exhausted as well. I was hoping we could console one another and be blessed with some hours of sleep. She struggled to get out of my arms when she realized I was removing her from Taittinger's room and carrying her to the top level of the house. I placed her on the bed, lay down beside her, and began caressing her. Her beautiful blue eyes were clouded with sadness.

I whispered softly to her, "Tatianna, I know how much you miss your playmate. It's so lonely without her. But Taittinger was so sick that she just could not be better. We'll never forget her, will we? You took such good care of her, and she loved to play with you every day. She is safe with God, my dear sweet Tatianna, and you are safe with me."

I fell asleep with Tatianna cradled in my right arm. But later, in the stillness of the night, I awoke, and she was gone. I knew she was back downstairs, waiting for Taittinger. I went to check on her and found her back on the bed, wide-eyed and so forlorn. I stayed with her the rest of the night.

This new routine continued for the next three days. Tatianna spent most of her days and nights downstairs. She wandered to the two upstairs levels for brief interludes—almost as though she were saying, "Let's make sure Taittinger is not hiding out somewhere else."

On the fourth night, I decided to return to my bedroom suite, but I did not force Tatianna to join me. When I awoke early the next morning, my dear sweet Tatianna was lying next to my heart. Perhaps the worst was over for her, but it was clear to me that she had loved and wanted to protect her companion and was capable of being overcome with grief.

Once again, I was back to a one-cat household with Tatianna at my side. Now, two precious orange marmalade cats, Noelle and Taittinger, had journeyed through our lives in less than two years. They left us with much love in our hearts, and their presence of spirit forever wafted in our midst.

Tatianna's Precious Little Playmate
Taittinger

Let's Go Shopping
Taittinger

The Pin Down
Tatianna and Taittinger

CHAPTER FOUR
TATIANNA AND
KATARINA—A LOVE TO
REMEMBER

**I am a part of all that I have touched
and that has touched me.**[1]
—Thomas Wolfe

Whenever I think of Tatianna, I simultaneously think of Katarina. The two of them were inseparable and had a fascinating long-term relationship. The depth of their affection, love, and concern for each other was so heartwarming.

Following Taittinger's death, Tatianna was sad and lost. She deeply mourned the loss of her loving companion. A friend of mine occasionally stayed at my home when she was in town on business trips. One morning I left the house first, and my friend later told me how Tatianna cried and wailed the minute I started the car engine and pulled out of the driveway. That image was heartbreaking. I knew Tatianna needed and deserved another furry friend to love. She had immeasurable love to give and spent hours alone while I was at work. I decided I wanted another orange marmalade kitten. I let my friends and clients know, and after several months of looking, I found what I hoped would be the perfect addition to our household. The kitten had golden amber eyes and was an orange marmalade domestic shorthair. I brought home the little orange kitten in the summer of 1988. It was with some trepidation that I introduced Tatianna to the new visitor. I hoped Tatianna would welcome her. It was, from the very beginning, a match made in heaven. As time went on, I believed that was literally true.

I initially dabbed Chloe perfume on both animals before I put them together, a trick I had learned in the pet business. (The philosophy behind this is that as the animals become familiar with each other's scents and realized they are the same, the odds of them accepting each other are increased.) It worked! Tatianna instinctively began mothering little Katarina, which was what I had named her after Olympic gold medal figure skater Katarina Witt. (I loved the name and also liked the idea of calling her "Katie" at times.) Katarina cried a lot as a kitten, and Tatianna was always checking up on her. Even though they had a loving and tender friendship, they liked to play aggressively. One time, Tattie was a little too rough with the kitten, and as a result, Tatianna's overzealous chewing left the tip of Katarina's left ear permanently bent!

Ken and Katarina took to one another immediately as well. One day, he decided to teach her to fetch. I knew cats could learn tricks, but I had never been successful in teaching them any. She quickly learned the game. He rolled up a tiny ball of paper, and when Katarina heard it rustling, she came running, because she knew that he would throw the paper ball. After he let it soar, she chased it down, batted it around the room for a while, carried it to him, and dropped it at his feet. Then the game started all over. Occasionally, she lost the paper ball under a piece of furniture. Then she looked like a contortionist, trying to retrieve her toy to take back to Ken. They kept this routine of throwing, batting, and retrieving the paper ball up until Katarina was panting like a dog. She loved this game. Sometimes, if she heard me accidentally making noises with paper, she ran over to me, expecting to play her game. I always stopped whatever I was doing and entertained her.

Katarina and Tatianna were inseparable; when you saw one, you invariably saw the other. They lay side by side and took turns washing and grooming each another. This ritual lasted for an indeterminable amount of time. They lay together like spoons, with their bodies nestled right next to each other. Other times, one laid her head on the other's back or tummy. They slept like that for hours. If a sound awakened one of them and she ran off to investigate, the other tagged along. And on rare occasions when Katarina was in a separate room and cried out, Tatianna ran from her spot to ensure her devoted friend was safe. Katarina did the same for Tatianna. It was one of the most touching rituals to observe between them. They were like each other's shadows, and each instinctively knew what was happening to the other. If I combed and brushed Tatianna, Katarina suddenly appeared. If I was petting and talking to Katarina, Tatianna heard me, regardless of where she was in the house. Then she ran in and wanted to join the activity. I was always amazed at how their feline ears detected even the quietest whispers.

Later in the summer of 1988, Ken and I traveled to England and Wales. I loved sharing some of my favorite English manors with Ken. He turned out to be a pro at navigating the roundabouts in England, and we had such fun looking for antiques in little villages for my shop. While we were gone, I boarded Tatianna and Katarina at my pet business. This was Katarina's first time being kept in a cage. We put Tatianna and Katarina in a large dog cage, so they had more room. They got along fine with this arrangement, and from that day forward, they always kept each other company in the same clinic kennel whenever I traveled. The hardest part about traveling for me was leaving Tatianna and Katarina behind. It was excruciating, and I pulled away from the clinic in tears. I missed them every day but took comfort knowing that our reunion would be jubilant.

When we returned from England, I started teaching part time at Northwood University. (My teaching career had started at Iowa State University many years before.) I had recently finished my MBA and desired to combine my love of academia with my entrepreneurial experience. Fortunately, a college specializing in business management was near where I lived, and I was thrilled with this opportunity. My schedule was full with the pet business and antiques store and teaching college courses. So Tatianna and Katarina had lots of time to spend together during my absence.

They played and roughhoused together. Occasionally, they enacted an aggressive game of hissing, swatting, and growling at one another. They circled each other, one waiting for the opportune moment to pin the other down. Tatianna was bigger and stronger and usually got the better of Katarina. But Katarina did have one effective move: grabbing on to Tatianna's neck with her two front paws and kicking her head repeatedly with her back legs. This rambunctious game lasted only a few minutes, and then they flopped down exhausted and began licking each other. Other times, the two of them sprinted through the house in wild pursuit. They slipped and slid on the polished wood floors and spun around corners. Sometimes, they even knocked themselves silly by running into pieces of furniture when they could not stop in time on the slick floors. These unexpected encounters with tables and chairs slowed them down only momentarily. They loved to play hide and seek, and each took great delight in jumping out from a secret spot to scare the wits out of the other. Sometimes I could swear that if I listened closely, I could almost hear the hider chuckling! Over the years as a spectator of their shenanigans, I always found them amusing; they never failed to elicit grins and laughter from me.

Their togetherness was not always all hustle and bustle. An indelible image in my mind is seeing their furry bodies curled up together on my bed, snugly and lovingly, in the shadows of the night. At this moment, I can close my eyes and see this sweet tableau as clearly as if it were yesterday.

Lazing in the Sun
Katarina

CHAPTER FIVE
TATIANNA'S FAVORITE SPOTS

Ah, there is nothing like staying home for real comfort.[1]
—Jane Austen

Tatianna loved her creature comforts, whether they were luxurious chairs, soft chenille pillows and throws, warm fuzzy blankets, or voluminous feather beds. And I blessed her with these accoutrements and more. She lived her entire life as strictly an indoor cat in a 1956 trilevel ranch-style house with rambling rooms, nooks and crannies, and lots of stairs. Tatianna reigned over the entire house, and she had several favorite spots where she loved to snuggle and slumber.

A guest bedroom, a guest bathroom, and a sports workout room, plus the infamous laundry room made up the downstairs level. The bedroom was decorated with antique oak furniture. The luxurious high bed was a fluffy feather bed, topped off with a white down comforter, and covered with numerous pillows of different shapes and sizes. Tatianna loved to while away the daytime hours here. She burrowed down into the comforter and rested against the pillows. Sometimes she hid under the pillows. The wooden oak blinds filtered in different levels of light, and an overhead fan provided a purr-fect sleeping atmosphere.

In her younger years, Tatianna jumped onto the bed with great ease. In her later years, she cleverly put her front paws on its wooden side rails and pulled herself up, or sometimes she hopped into the antique wicker doll buggy, which was next to the bed, and from there was able to reach her destination. There was a soft towel in the bottom of the buggy, which welcomed her to sleep there all day after she had jumped in. The sides and hood of the carriage also provided a private sleeping spot. Many times, Katarina joined Tatianna and a doll in the buggy. It was so cozy in there that not another creature or toy could possibly fit.

The bed and buggy were not the room's only fascination. The room also had a comfy wingback chair whose seat cushion was so soft that a person literally sank down into it. I often found Tatianna in this chair, especially in cooler weather. The high back and arms provided a sense of security and warmth. Next to the wingback, there was a small round table with an embroidered tablecloth, which provided a safe, dark hideaway for Tatianna. The tip of her gray tail was the only giveaway that she was there.

One way to access the house was at the front of the guest bedroom. When I pulled into the driveway, I typically used this convenient entrance. I quickly developed the habit of looking down at the door's base as I unlocked it. If Tatianna and Katarina were snoozing in this room, they usually both welcomed me right at the door. These blessed moments always brought me great joy.

The guest bath, with its cool white tile floor, was a welcoming relief to Tatianna on warm summer days. In the winter, she thought it was fun to lie on the soft chenille floor rugs. And, of course, she had to occasionally peek behind the shower curtain—just in case someone had left a slow trickle of water to play in or to drink from!

The workout and baseball memorabilia room had evolved over the years from a den and home office. In the later years of Tatianna's life, it was a sports room equipped with exercise machines. She liked to lie in a soft black leather recliner and watch each of my movements with great intensity. A velour sports throw was tossed over one side of the chair, and I often found it rearranged and Tatianna snuggled up in it. Other times, she just knocked the throw on the floor and slept on it there.

So many attractions drew and kept Tatianna in the lower level of the house. But with twenty-four hours in a day, she had many more rooms to visit. Seven steep steps led to the middle level of the house. Tatianna and Katarina always greeted me at the top of the landing if they had been in the upper part of the house. They had just enough time to reach this location after they heard my car pull in the driveway. Tatianna would sit up erectly, and Katarina would straddle a narrow ledge along the right side of the steps. Sometimes they sat side by side as if they were posing for a photograph. I often heard them hit the floor running from the upper level as I walked in the downstairs door. I would chuckle; they always wanted to beat me to that spot on the stairs—and they always did! They loved to greet me, and I loved seeing four bright eyes looking at me. As I made my way to the top of the stairs, Tatianna rubbed against my legs, and Katarina meowed for dinner.

In the kitchen on the floor beneath the wall oven were two red placemats topped with their red, black, and white food and water bowls. The kitchen was, of course, the room where they always ate as often and as much as they could!

The kitchen floor was also an appropriate place to look for some scrumptious crumbs, and occasionally they ran their noses over the floor like vacuum sweepers, looking for tidbits.

From the kitchen, you enter what was undoubtedly Tatianna's favorite room of the house. The dining room was a light, open, airy sunroom with five sets of windows on the room's northern and eastern side. A glass door led to a courtyard on the southern side, and a door led to the backyard and patio on the northern side. So there was great visibility of the outside world—especially for an indoor cat. I furnished the room in vintage white wicker, including two rocking chairs and two straight-armed chairs. Plush pillows accented all of the chairs. A small table covered with a white tablecloth and a glass top stood between the straight-armed chairs. This table was a cool spot on warm summer days, and the raised elevation provided a perfect vantage point for Tatianna to see outside. For more than a dozen years of Tatianna's life, the dining room table also had a glass top. Although discouraged, Tatianna still made a habit to spend time on the glass-topped dining table.

In later years, I acquired an early 1900s oval mahogany table with inlay. To Tatianna, the wood felt almost as good as the glass top. Sometimes, she hung out on the soft velveteen upholstered dining room chairs. She also thought the rug under the table was not such a bad spot either! But the wicker chairs were the most popular. When Tatianna lay in one of the rocking chairs facing the kitchen, she could watch my every movement in the kitchen. When in the other rocking chair, she could see outside the eastern glass windows. The birdbath sitting by the corner of the house fascinated her. She especially liked to watch the screeching blue jays take a bath. One of the wicker chairs on the northern side was directly in line with the glass door, so she could see what was happening in the courtyard. A fun feature of the room was a six-inch ledge around the windows, and her common practice was to race around the ledge while eyeing something outside that was unreachable—perhaps a neighbor's cat or a squirrel.

At night, the room became enchanted. The white lights in the courtyard as well as the gazebo and the patio were visible. The night creatures, such as raccoons and opossums, stirred her. Often there was a light breeze blowing through the room, and you could hear wind chimes lightly striking on the patio. I often turned out all of the lamps and sat there with Tatianna. I understood why she enjoyed it so much.

The dining room opened into the living room. This room had an eight-foot picture window with a wide windowsill. I dressed the window with white lace curtains that fluttered in the typically cool South Floridian breeze. Tatianna loved to sit on the windowsill and look at the plants in front of the window. She could watch lizards and hear and see people walking by. Early in the morning, she could bathe in the eastern sunbeams coming through the window. I furnished the room with a leather Queen Anne loveseat, wingback chairs, and a Victorian walnut rocking chair. Normally on the weekend, Tatianna came to the foot of the rocking chair and looked up at me as I sat in front of the picture window with my morning tea. She placed her paws on the edge of the seat, and I lifted her up on my lap. She lay there and enjoyed the quiet rocking. It was always a very special time for us. I had covered the leather couch with needlepoint pillows; often I found Tatianna curled up next to them. She gave the wingback chair equal time, and she also liked to lie on the rug by the front door. Generally, the front door was kept open because of the louvered screen door. Tatianna enjoyed sniffing at the door to figure out who had been a visitor the night before—most likely the neighbor's cat.

She was fascinated by cardboard boxes and loved to hide and sleep in them and to lie on them. So generally, the living room and dining room décor included at least one box, which remained until it became old and tattered; then a new one appeared and Tatianna soon broke it in. The room also had a baby grand piano with a bench covered in a concealing throw. Tatianna and Katarina often played hide-and-seek under it.

I spent many waking and snoozing hours in the living room with Tatianna draped across my lap. She kept me company as I read numerous newspapers and magazines, graded hundreds of college term papers, and prepared lecture notes over the years. This room also had a great view from the couch into the dining room, so Tatianna could watch me move around. But the minute I sat down, she was by my side or in my lap.

From the living room, there were five steps leading to the hallway of the upper level. Three doors led off of the hall—one to the violet sitting room, one to the pansy bathroom, and the other to the master suite, bath, and home office. The hall landing served as another one of Tatianna's welcome-me-home spots, particularly when she was in one of the upper-level rooms. She got up from wherever she had been sleeping, went to the hall, and looked down into the living room as I entered that room. It warmed my heart to have her greet me!

The violet room had a southern exposure with a light, airy feel and often had refreshing breezes blowing through the wispy, white lace curtains. Vintage white wicker and violet floral wallpaper decorated the room. Tatianna's favorite spot was an oversized wicker chair with fluffy cushions. I tossed a purple chenille throw over one side of the chair, which was covered partially with cushions. It was a wonderful spot for her to snuggle! Depending on the time of the day, Tatianna could catch some sun in this room as well. The driveway was just below the window, and this special spot was ideal for her to hear my arrival home. This room was one of my favorites as well. I often had my early-morning tea there on workdays or relaxed there later with a book. Invariably, Tatianna was in my lap or stretched out on the needlepoint rug in front of me. She simply loved being where I was—and Katarina was never far behind.

The pansy bathroom was across the hall from the violet room. One of Tatianna's favorite games was to play between the shower curtain and liner while I was showering. She jumped up on the edge of the tub and walked along the rim. Sometimes, she peeked out when she reached one end or the other. Katarina stayed on the vanity counter, looking around the corner toward the tub and keeping watch. So I seldom showered alone! The two remained in the small bathroom with me until I left for another part of the house; then they followed along in tandem. Tatianna also liked to crawl into the tub and drink water from the very slow-leaking faucet. I could always tell where she had been if I reached down to pet her and the top of her head was wet. Sometimes, she even lay in the tub and napped. Other times, it was much more fun to mischievously shred the toilet paper with her teeth. She could literally destroy a roll in minutes. Sometimes I found a pile on the floor with fragments hanging from the remaining roll or from her mouth!

The master bedroom suite was home to Tatianna for one-third of her life, because she slept with me just about every night. Parallel to the bed was a six-foot mahogany dresser. In her younger days, Tatianna liked to jump from the bed to the dresser. She knew I stored catnip in one of the drawers. As she aged, she was not as confident about making the leap. The dresser was in line with a window, so the top of it was a terrific vantage point to catch a glimpse of a squirrel or bird. The master suite also included my office and sitting area at the opposite end of the room. The soft, cushioned velvet chair in the sitting area, as well as the needlepoint chair at the dressing table, was a common lounging spot for Tatianna. She often lay on a rug under my desk from where she could see me at the far end of the room.

Of course, making up the bed with fresh linens was a highlight of our day. After fluffing up the feather bed, Katarina and Tatianna entertained themselves by jumping around on the bed. I joined in their games by putting the fitted sheet on the bed with them underneath it. Generally, Tatianna crawled out, but Katarina liked to stay underneath the fitted sheet until Tatianna noticed the lump. Then Tatianna pawed at the raised area and followed it as Katarina burrowed like a mole. Eventually, Katarina reached the end of the bed and jumped onto the floor. I always had a good laugh watching their antics.

Tatianna liked to snuggle—especially during cool nights, when she would curl up next to me. Katarina sidled next to Tatianna. I could make out the outlines of their bodies in the shadows of the night. Tatianna, until the latter part of her life, was the larger cat. The texture of her fur was shorter and thicker. Katarina's fur was longer and softer. So I could tell who was nearby without looking. I could not move or turn over without disturbing them. Sometimes, I cradled them both in my arms, and other times they draped themselves across my feet. They slept until I got up, because fortunately they learned as kittens that I was not going to feed them at 5:00 AM.

Our morning ritual included Tatianna and Katarina coming back to the master suite immediately after breakfast, where they observed me getting ready to leave for work. Sometimes, they crawled back into bed. And many a time, I told them, "What a special life you have!" They could always sense that I was leaving soon, and I hated telling them good-bye every morning. But I always made it a special ritual to pet each of them and tell them I loved them. I also told them what time I would be home. Depending on my day schedule at the pet business and my night classes, Tatianna and Katarina had eight to twelve hours to roam the house freely. But I could always count on Tatianna and Katarina to greet me when I got home. As I turned into my driveway after each absence, I jumped out of the car with door key in hand. I could not wait to unlock the house to see where Tatianna and Katarina were waiting for me—by the door, at the top of the stair landing, or on the upper level. It did not matter where they were as I always embraced both of them and told them how much I had missed them. What a glorious, blessed moment to be reunited with loved ones at the end of the day!

What do you think?
Tatianna and Katarina

CHAPTER SIX
TATIANNA'S OUTDOOR
ESCAPADE

It's not so much what happens.
It is what one does when it happens
that really counts.[1]
—Laura Ingalls Wilder

Tatianna's most frightening escape (at least to me) occurred one evening when I was leaving the house. She was lounging on the downstairs guest bed.

"I will be back in a few minutes, my sweet Tattie. I am going to pick up a pizza," I called out.

I turned around and gathered up my purse and keys. As I opened the door, Tatianna came from out of nowhere and bolted out the door. A straight path ahead led to my car and the street. A left turn would have taken her into a high retaining wall along the driveway. Instead, she went right and flew up four cement steps and was gone from my sight before I could utter a word. The action stunned me; Tatianna had never done anything like this. I ran up the steps after her, but there was no glimpse of her, nor was there any sound of her. She had quickly and simply vanished.

A wood fence separated my backyard property from the neighbors. I ran to my backyard, hoping to find her there. I did not see her anywhere. I frantically called her name. I left my yard, ran over to the neighbor's side of the fence, and still did not find Tatianna. My heart was pounding, and I was breathing hard. I heard barking dogs from the street behind me, and I became even more frightened for her safety. My mind whirled with thoughts of the outdoor peril that could befall Tatianna at any moment. She had been safely sheltered inside the house through-out her life and did not know how to survive in the outside world. I had to quickly find her before she got hit by a car, attacked by an animal, or catnapped. I reminded myself to breathe deeply and to get control of the situation.

I ran back to the house, grabbed my car keys, and jumped into the car. I slowly drove around the block, but I did not see a single animal. The barking dogs had quieted down. I returned home and decided that walking around the block might be more fruitful, because it was dusk and hard to see clearly from the street. I walked past my next-door neighbor's house and rounded the bend, passing the house that sits on the corner between two blocks. There was no Tatianna, and there were no people out walking to ask if they had seen a gray cat. As I approached the first house on the street behind my house, I looked up the steps leading to the front door. To my amazement, Tatianna lay on the second step from the front-door landing.

I stopped dead in my tracks. My first thought was that she would run if I dashed up the steps. So I slowly ascended the first of the twelve steps that led to her. I talked softly to her.

"Tattie, what in the world are you doing out here?"

Tatianna just lay there looking at me with her eyes that were as big as saucers. Due to low light, her pupils had engulfed her eyes.

"Dear God, please just keep her on that step," I silently prayed.

Slowly I moved up the second step, then the third, and the fourth. I continued speaking to Tatianna quietly and reassuringly.

"Tattie, it's time I carried you back home. There are doggies out here, and I do not want you to get hurt."

No one was around, and I again prayed that no one would walk by or come out of the door suddenly. After what seemed like an eternity, I was close enough to reach down and grab Tatianna. I scooped her up in my arms and cradled her close to me.

"Oh, my dear sweet Tatianna, I thought I had lost you and would never see you again."

Fortunately, she did not struggle to get out of my arms. I knew we had had a narrow escape, and she had used up another life. We returned home. After I gave her a bath to remove dirt and leaves from her coat, we settled into bed and gave thanks. We had been blessed that the outcomes I had worried about had not come to pass.

I will never know what possessed Tatianna to run out of the house. Although she was always curious around open doors her whole life, Tatianna never ran out again. All in all, she was probably missing less than ten minutes. But for me, it was an eternity—one of the most frantic and fearful times of my life. As for Tatianna, the best conclusion I ever came to was that she just wanted to see if the grass really *was* greener on the other side of the fence.

CHAPTER SEVEN
TATIANNA'S UNWELCOME
SUNDAY VISITOR

**What a wonderful day I think,
turning it over in my hand to its starting point again.**[1]
—Anne Morrow Lindbergh

One Sunday afternoon as I walked through the dining room, I caught Tatianna snoozing in one of the vintage wicker rocking chairs. She was burrowed into a soft blue chenille cushion. Tatianna, Katarina, and I had just enjoyed a late breakfast, and a lazy Sunday afternoon stretched before us. But to my horror, I also saw a fat, black snake coiled up along the baseboard just under the windows on the eastern side of the house! In this room, the northern and eastern sides of the room are all jalousie windows covering more than three-fourths of the wall height. The windows and screens are original to the house; some of the screens have small tears and holes in them. I figured the snake had crawled through one of the old screens.

I stopped dead in my tracks and did not make a sound. A second look at the snake told me that it was probably more than three feet long when uncoiled. Tatianna was approximately one yard from the intruder. Apparently, neither had discovered the other. I immediately knew that I had to get Tatianna out of the room and as far away from the snake as possible. Then I would find a way to deal with the snake. I quietly and cautiously tiptoed over to within arm's length of Tatianna's chair. I reached out and snatched her up in my arms and swiftly deposited her behind a nearby kitchen door. I glanced around the rest of the dining room, and I was thankful that oddly enough Katarina was nowhere to be seen.

Now, my next feat was to get the snake back outside, where it belonged, without causing a ruckus! Fortunately, I do not go into hysterics whenever I see one. I am accustomed to seeing them in my yard. Calmly and methodically, I grabbed a broom and dust mop out of the kitchen closet and crept back into the dining room. The snake was still in the same position, which was over twenty feet from the back door. I placed the broom in my right hand and the mop in my left hand. I stood about a yard from the snake and stretched, sandwiching him between the broom and mop. I successfully escorted the snake out the back door with the broom and mop and flung him into the back corner of the yard, far away from the house!

Keeping true to form, Tatianna was loudly meowing and banging on the closed door while I was moving the snake. She knew that she was missing something exciting and was doing her best to recapture my attention. I opened the kitchen door and carried her back to her comfy chair. She settled back down into its softness and gave me a look as if to say, "What was *that* all about?"

I must say I really *was* frightened as I entertained all of the possible scenarios after the unwelcome Sunday afternoon visitor was gone. What would have happened if I had not discovered the snake when I did? What if Tatianna had attacked the snake and been bitten? What if Katarina had been disturbed by the noise and come to investigate? What if the snake had crawled to another room of the house without me knowing it? I thanked God for watching over all of us and keeping us safe in our home. Once again, the situation reminded me of why a cat is blessed with nine lives. Tatianna's guardian angel was truly watching over her that day!

Don't Wake Me Now
Tatianna

CHAPTER EIGHT
TATIANNA'S RELATIONSHIP
WITH LINDA

**Each friend represents a world in us,
a world possibly not born until they arrive
and it is only by this meeting that a new world is born.**[1]
—Anaïs Nin

My life dramatically changed in the fall of 1989. On November 4, my beloved Ken was in a motorcycle accident as he turned into a parking lot at his workplace. A dairy tanker truck ran a red light and struck him. Despite serious injuries, six hours in surgery, and one week spent in intensive care, the prognosis for Ken was good. His doctors had suggested he would be home for Thanksgiving. I was planning a welcome-home celebration.

During the two weeks of Ken's hospitalization, Tatianna kept a constant vigil at my side whenever I dragged myself home, emotionally and physically spent. She crawled up into my lap and rubbed her head against my head and shoulders. She nestled into my arms and rested there for as long as I could possibly stand to sit still. She was a centering force for me during what was unfolding as the most painful, heart-wrenching experience of my life. She lay next to my heart licking the tears off my cheeks as I cried myself to sleep. If I got up in the middle of a sleepless night, she followed me as I meandered aimlessly through the house. Sometimes we ended up downstairs in the guest bedroom, eventually falling asleep together in the comforting, oversized, wingback chair. Other nights, we sat together in the dining room in the early morning hours, listening to the fascinating and calming sounds of nature emanating from my backyard paradise. Tatianna sensed my fear and my heartache. My worry and concern could not be masked from my furry and intuitive companion. The steady solace Tatianna provided me gave me the strength and courage each day to face whatever was ahead. And there was a lot more to be endured.

So when the call came during the end of the second week of hospitalization, it was totally unexpected. Ken and I had spent the evening together at the hospital—laughing, joking, and talking about the future. Ken was amusing me with attorney jokes. We reminisced about our recent summer trip to London and planned our next trip to London. I departed from the hospital around 9:00 PM. Less than two hours later, I was back. On Saturday, November 18, 1989, at 10:30 PM, a hospital nurse contacted me at home. Her exact words, "Mr. Kraft has taken a turn for the worse," will forever ring in my ears. In a mere instant, my life's course changed forever.

When I got to the hospital a few minutes later, Ken had already passed away. An undetected embolism had traveled from his right leg to his lungs. I sat with him in his room for more than an hour. I kept replaying in my mind our evening together. I tried to piece together the conversation as though it would change the outcome. I kept repeating the words, "I love you," which had been our final exchange when I left. We had always closed every telephone conversation and every departure the past four years with those thoughts. Tonight had been no different. I was struck with the irony that Ken's passion was riding motorcycles, and that was what led to his passing. In retrospect, the doctors were right about Ken being home for Thanksgiving—however, it was not the "home" that I had expected. Many years later, I can vividly recall one of his doctors telling me as we stood at the foot of Ken's bed that my life would never be the same. I thought that was a strange thing to say to me. Of course, in the end, the doctor was right.

My friends and colleagues were kind and generous. My business partner was the first person at my home early Sunday morning and later sat with me at visitation, holding my hand. A colleague offered to proctor final exams for me, and my academic dean attended the funeral. All of the neighbors on the street came to my home the evening following Ken's death, bringing food and friendship. My family, thousands of miles away, called several times a day. Ken's supervisor from work came to my home Monday evening and just sat with me for hours. Ken's first cousin called often. Ken was buried the day before Thanksgiving. My neighbor Mary Jo supported me at the cemetery. A couple hundred people—the same congregation of family, friends, and colleagues who were to have assembled for our wedding—celebrated Ken's life. I buried my heart that day.

The days and weeks following Ken's death, I simply existed. The vision of my life had not included this dead-end street. I felt as though I had actually driven off a cliff and was free-falling. At the time, I thought the only person who could possibly save me had tragically been removed from my life. I was also dealing with a monumental change at work. My business partner had decided to go to law school, so we had been seeking a buyer for the pet care store. My long-standing thirteen-year partnership in the business came to an end in early January 1990, when we sold it. With it gone and Ken's death, my professional, personal, and social foundation had literally dissolved in a six-week period. I was devastated, distraught, and disillusioned. I walked around—or more precisely, sat around—in a daze.

I rarely left the house unless it was to go to the attorney's office or to check on Ken's two teenage sons. I taught one class at Northwood University in the winter that just met once a week. However, it would take me days to prepare one lecture because I could not focus. I had no appetite, interest in life, or energy. I lost fifteen pounds. I slipped into the depths of despair.

The sleepless nights were soon replaced with sleeping around the clock. Sleep became an escape and refuge for me. Tatianna, once again, found a way to help me by simply being wherever I was. And if that meant spending twelve or more hours a day in the bedroom with me, then that was what she did. Sometimes, she snuggled close to me and rested in the crook of my legs. Sometimes, she stretched across my feet. Other times, she slept in my arms. Even if she lay on the rug in my office area at the far end of the bedroom suite, her mere physical presence in the same room calmed and soothed me.

When I was not sleeping for indeterminable hours, I rocked away the day in a Victorian chair in the living room. The chair sat in front of the expansive picture window, giving me a well-needed dose of sunshine and a view of the flowering shrubs. Occasionally, I heard voices from the sidewalk as neighbors passed by on their daily walks. Without fail, I found Tatianna at my feet, ceremoniously rubbing her paws on the tops of my shoes. She amused and entertained me. Sometimes, she rolled over on her back with her four paws pointing toward the ceiling. At other times, she tussled with Katarina or played with toys. Once in a while, I remembered to play fetch with Katarina, as Ken had done. She remembered how to play it with me. I rolled up a tiny ball of paper tightly and then threw it as far across the room as possible. She then sprinted to find it and enjoyed swatting it around before bringing back to me. It was quite a sight for Tatianna and me to watch. As I reenacted Ken's game, I sensed his adventurous spirit, and it always brought a smile to my face.

Tatianna had an ongoing repertoire of joy to share and was destined to draw on it indefinitely for my benefit and healing. Sometimes, the only sound in these quiescent moments was Tatianna's familiar, contented purr echoing in the utter silence of the room. Sometimes, she basked in the dappled sunlight, filtering through the lace curtains. Other times, she crawled up in my lap, and we rocked together for hours. I held her, caressed her, and told her how much I missed Ken. I sobbed uncontrollably, but she never left my sight. She stayed at her post as a sentinel, taking me in with her absorbing and understanding eyes. Despite my dazed state, I could not help but sense her heartfelt devotion.

Watching the antics of Katarina and Tatianna was a healthy diversion for me. They helped me to forget my sorrow for a few moments. They were also quick to remind me of mealtimes—in particular, theirs. The mere act of filling a water bowl and opening a can of cat food several times a day became an integral part of my healing process. They were teaching me that in the midst of death, there is also life. They helped me to see the value of focusing on the present—that it is time to eat! By living in that moment with them and watching them enjoy their food, I was not thinking about the pain from the past or worrying about the uncertainty of the future. After the mealtime ritual, they meticulously and methodically washed each other. The first time I saw them behave this way, I thought it was the most tenderhearted gesture I had ever seen. First, Tatianna groomed Katarina, working her way from her head to tail. Then, they reversed the roles, and Katarina would fastidiously return the favor. I just sat and watched in awe the ordinariness yet sacredness of these moments. When the bathing was over, they took one of their many daily naps. They experimented with different positions until both were totally comfortable. And then once again, their purring duet resonated in the sorrowful silence.

I filled the early years following Ken's death with working through the grieving process, handling his estate as his personal representative, overseeing a successful wrongful death lawsuit on his behalf, and serving as the guardian of his seventeen-year-old. During this juncture of my life, I clearly understood why God had lent Tatianna to me. She was playing her role faultlessly. I did not know it then, but God would give me the opportunity to be Tatianna's lifeline many years later.

My master suite actually became a restorative retreat that sheltered me from the outside world. Surrounded by my beloved Tatianna and Katarina, my favorite books, my lecture notes, and my students' projects, I was able to reflect and quietly contemplate what had transpired in my life. The teaching and interacting with the students at Northwood University was my outside lifeline. Preparing for my special students a couple of times each week gave me a much needed mental diversion. Attending occasional university events was a much-needed social diversion. Tatianna was my inside lifeline. Clearly, as a result of sharing Ken's tragedy, Tatianna and I grew infinitely closer. Our bond deepened, and our communication took on a higher form. She helped to diminish my sense of loneliness and anguish on this journey of grief that to me seemed to have no stop sign in sight. Simply sitting and lying quietly with me for hours, followed by weeks, months, and years, Tatianna shared my sorrow. Although she was incapable of speaking a word as a human visitor could, her silent communication was profound. Without uttering a word, Tatianna spoke to my soul with her sparkling, penetrating blue eyes. She was clearly journeying with me—wherever we went and for as long as it took. She gave me the gift of hope, and without hope, I could not have endured my days. She was with me as I reclaimed my strength and passion for life. The light of Tatianna's soul had forever captured my heart. And it was with heartfelt gratitude that I offered up a prayer of thanksgiving for this marvelous feline companion. Although I had lost a physical life with Ken, God had set aside this precious interlude for Tatianna and me. It was life altering for both of us. So I made the turn: My faith in God; an understanding that this too shall pass; and the devoted love, tenderness, and companionship of Tatianna sustained me.

Warm and Snuggly
Tatianna and Katarina

CHAPTER NINE
TATIANNA AND THE
THANKSGIVING GUEST

Another cat? Perhaps. For love, there is also a season
its seed must be resown. But a family cat
is not replaceable like a worn out coat or set of tires.
Each new kitten becomes its own cat
and none is repeated.
I am four cats old, measuring out my life
in friends that have succeeded,
but not replaced one another. [1]
—Irving Townsend

For a brief time, I had a three-cat family. In the fall of 1991, a stray black cat began hanging around my house. In the beginning, I really did not think much about the visitor. My enclosed backyard was a haven for all kinds of animals, including raccoons, opossums, squirrels, and neighborhood cats. The neighbors' cats of assorted breeds passed through my yard on a regular basis to aggravate Tatianna and Katarina, who could see them from the dining room. Sometimes, the visitors blatantly walked along the brick ledge outside the dining room as the two inside cats followed them inside the windowsill. It was always a comical sight. They hissed at one another and batted their paws against the windows to no avail. The outside cats could not get in, and the inside cats could not get out.

After a while, the stray black cat constantly appeared out of nowhere and was wherever I was. It was eerie. She joined me on the patio chair if I sat down. If I went for a walk, she walked companionably along behind me like a dog. She slept on my front stoop at night. She slept in a brick planter recessed under the house overhang whenever it rained. When I came home, she ran from the next-door neighbor's house or from a house across the street to greet me. The first time I saw her scamper across the heavily traveled street when I pulled into my driveway, I feared for her safety. After a very short time of shadowing me, the stray had worked her way into my heart.

No one knew whether she had an owner or a home. My next-door neighbor Mary Jo told me that she was feeding the black kitty daily. Although the cat seemed to be at my house most of the time, I had resisted feeding her. The cat looked incredibly healthy for an outdoor cat that apparently fended for herself.

On Thanksgiving morning in 1991, I scurried around the house to get ready for a special holiday with Joe, an old friend with whom I had reconnected. We had both attended the University of Missouri more than twenty years ago, and we had socialized with the same group of friends, but we had never dated each other. We had always kept in touch, and a couple of business trips had brought him to my part of the world over the decades. After Ken passed away, I contacted Joe to let him know. He was living in Los Angeles at the time and was getting ready to move to White Plains, New York. Later in the fall of 1991, Joe began flying monthly to West Palm Beach. I had never been in a long-distance relationship, so even though I had a lot to learn, I planned to make every moment count when we were together, which was my intention for our first Thanksgiving holiday. However, my cats had another plan in mind.

As I opened the back door that led from the dining room to the patio, the stray black cat sprinted inside in a flash. Tatianna and Katarina were in the dining room, and pandemonium erupted. My two cats simultaneously attacked the stray cat. They stunned the Thanksgiving visitor with their unkind welcome. After a lot of screaming, I managed to pull Tatianna and Katarina away long enough to chase the stray cat outside. Although their response saddened me, I was not surprised. Tatianna and Katarina simply had to protect their territory. They had clearly sent me a message, and this episode squelched any remote notion of mine to adopt this cat and bring her into my loving household.

A couple of hours later, Joe arrived. By then, Tatianna and Katarina had settled down, and the stray black cat was nowhere to be seen. Joe chuckled as I told the story in vivid detail.

Joe did not have any pets, so having to constantly vie with two cats for my attention was definitely a new experience. Tatianna, of course, made it easy for him by climbing into his lap and gazing up at him with her saucer-like blue eyes. She was incredibly comfortable around Joe. Katarina was more skittish, and it took several years for her to get accustomed to his company. Joe fed the cats and played with them. He always asked about them when he called. It was clear to me that he understood my cats were family, and he treated them as such.

Several more months went by, and the stray cat did not leave the premises. Although she did not try to get back into the house, she was still constantly by my side whenever I was outside. I was becoming more attached and agonized about her life situation—outside in a metropolitan area. At the same time, I did not want to emotionally traumatize my indoor cats by introducing a third animal or risk a serious medical threat to them because strays were prey to numerous diseases. So I struggled philosophically and morally with this dilemma.

One evening, some circumstances beyond my control made the decision for me. I came home from work, and the familiar black cat met me in the driveway, limping. Upon closer examination, I saw that she had been in a catfight and had an abscess. I immediately called my veterinarian and took her to the clinic. The doctor gave me medicine for her, and I brought her back home, where I found myself medicating her whenever she appeared on the patio. Of course, the bond between us grew deeper. Shortly after her full recovery, I decided to try to integrate her into our established feline household. The veterinarian gave her a medical examination, and the groomer bathed and dipped her for fleas. In fact, she almost died from an allergic reaction to the flea dip. It took her more than three days to completely wake up and become alert after the dipping. During that time, I kept her in the guest bedroom with the door shut. She slept on the featherbed. Of course, Tatianna and Katarina suspected something unusual was going on. I used the perfume trick when I first put them together, but it did not work as it had with Tatianna and Katarina years ago. Marnie, the stray who was named after an Alfred Hitchcock movie, thought the guest room was hers. After all, she had been alone for days, resting and recuperating from her near-death experience with the dip, and suddenly, two monsters invaded her territory. And, of course, Tatianna and Katarina thought they had to protect their territory—which just happened to be the whole house. After all, they had lived this way forever. It was a serious error in judgment.

For several weeks, I kept Marnie separated from Tatianna and Katarina. At night, I let Marnie out of the upstairs violet room, and all of us were together. I could referee, if necessary. In time, Tatianna and Katarina learned to tolerate Marnie, and they could be together when I was away. At night, the four of us slept together, but Marnie was always a shadow visible at a far-off corner of the bed. The three of them never really developed a loving and harmonious bond, because sadly, Tatianna and Katarina always viewed Marnie as an interloper.

About six months after Marnie had settled into inside living, Mary Jo made a confession that we would laugh about for years to come.

"Do you remember me telling you I fed the black cat when she lived outside?" she asked.

"Oh, yes! That was so kind of you," I responded.

"Well, it is true I was feeding the cat, but I was feeding her at *your* house, and not my house," she said.

I burst out laughing. "Well, no wonder Marnie adopted *me*. I did not have a chance!"

Just like Tatianna, Marnie had help in making her way to my doorstep.

Marnie spent many of her indoor days draped over one end of the baby grand piano near the picture window. With the higher vantage point, she could survey her previous outdoor dominion. The birds lighting on the shrubs and the chameleons sunning on the window ledge entertained her. She seemed content being on the inside looking out. I never had to worry about her sneaking out. She easily adapted to indoor living and to my lifestyle. She watched me leave for work and patiently waited for my return. She loved to curl up in my lap and to sleep with me.

Marnie was extremely affectionate with me, and I always referred to her as "my little angel kitty." She had arrived in my yard during a time when I was grieving Ken's death, and she knew how to pull on my heartstrings. I knew God had loaned her to me to fulfill a purpose, and she did it in the most loving way. She was persistent and did not allow the numerous obstacles to deter her from her mission. But her mission was not yet completed.

On Friday evening, December 25, 1992, I received a shocking phone call that my father had suffered a heart attack and lapsed into a coma. I had spoken with my mother that morning, but I had not talked with my father because he was not feeling well. The next day, I finalized plans to return to the Midwest and found a friend to come to my home everyday to care for Tatianna, Katarina, and Marnie.

All the way home on the airplane, I kept praying to God to let me get to my father's bedside in time. I kept repeating over and over, "Daddy, I'm on my way. Daddy, I'm on my way. Please wait for me." My mind teemed with thoughts of my father. My father was a fierce competitor, and baseball was his life's passion. As a teenager, he traveled, usually hitchhiking, to Catalina Island in California to play winter baseball with the hopes of being signed by a major league team. During the three winters of 1937–39 when he played in California, he sent postcards back to his parents in Missouri, which are fascinating to read. He also attended the Roger Dean All-Star Baseball School in Hot Springs, Arkansas, in 1938. But life threw him a big, fat curveball, and he spent four years and seven months in the U.S. Army, fighting in the Pacific Rim during World War II. When he returned home in 1947, he was twenty-eight years old, and his dream of a professional ball career was no longer on the horizon. He returned to Missouri, got married, and started farming. In 1950, I was born and named after my father's favorite song.

However, his love of the game never diminished despite the detour. He coached winning Little League and Pony League teams. He spent thousands of hours playing ball with my two brothers. He traveled to my older brother's college baseball games and watched my younger brother in American Legion games. In later years, he umpired softball games all over northeast Missouri. He was an avid St. Louis Cardinals and Baltimore Orioles fan and listened to all of their games on the radio and later watched them on television. He knew every statistic of every player.

From what I can determine from newspaper accounts and people's stories, he was a talented baseball player. In particular, he was a phenomenal hitter who was scouted by the Chicago Cubs. I remember sitting with him in front of the television and watching Stan Musial's retirement ceremony in 1963. The famous St. Louis Cardinal had won seven National League batting titles in his twenty-two-year career. As we watched, tears streamed down my father's face. And although I was only a teenager, I realized he truly believed he could have been that caliber of player with that kind of notoriety—if only life had gone differently. Although we will never know for sure, I believe it, too. I know my competitive spirit comes from my father. He taught me to go for what I wanted in life and to try to accomplish what I was destined to do. But he also taught me that life took unexpected turns.

I arrived in Quincy, Illinois, on Sunday afternoon. My cousin, Alan, met me at the airport and took me immediately to the hospital in Keokuk, Iowa. My mother, two brothers, and sister-in-law had been at the hospital since late Christmas night. My sister and her husband had arrived on Saturday. Everyone was exhausted. My father's condition had not changed. He was hooked up to every imaginable machine, and I could do nothing but silently weep when I saw him. I took his hand in mine, squeezed it, and told him I had made it. What a bittersweet reunion it was. Sometimes, you got to be with your loved one at the end; sometimes, you did not. I was grateful I could be there with my father. Approximately two hours after my arrival, my seventy-three-year-old father passed away in the presence of his entire loving family.

Once again death had visited me. Death does not discriminate; it can call any day of the year, holiday or otherwise. Just about seven years ago, I had said good-bye to Noelle right after Thanksgiving. Just three years ago, I had said good-bye to Ken the day before Thanksgiving. Five days after Christmas, I was telling my father good-bye. It was almost more than I could fathom, much less bear.

On December 30, we laid my father to rest in a small church cemetery in rural Missouri that was surrounded by farmland, pastures, and animals. The day was freezing cold, snowy, and stark, but beautiful. As the military gun saluted my father and the flag laid over his coffin was folded, a cow mooed, punctuating with ordinariness the extraordinary day for me. Some profound moments are etched in your mind forever.

I returned to Florida a week later. Tatianna and Katarina met me at the top of the kitchen stairs. Marnie was not far behind. They were deliriously happy to see me. I gathered them up in my arms and hugged and kissed them. This reunion was so sweet. To be reunited with loved ones again—what more could I ever want? I fell into bed and stayed there for several days. The tiredness was reminiscent of the days following Ken's death. I simply could not move. Tatianna, Katarina, and Marnie barely left my side the first night back. They waited patiently for me to stir out of bed the next morning and plod down to the kitchen to feed them. They sat at my feet while I sipped my tea. Then they followed me back to bed. We kept up this routine for several days until I finally returned to work.

A couple weeks later, I received a photograph of my father, opening the Christmas gift I had sent him—a shiny blue pen. He was holding the pen in his hand and smiling—just a few hours before his heart attack. Later, my mother gave the pen back to me. I placed it in my memento drawer, and it remained there for almost ten years—until I wrote his story for Tatianna's book.

Although my father and Tatianna had only spent a few days around each other during his only Florida visit, they quickly had become best buddies. In retrospect, I am thankful I got to share one of my life's passions—my love of cats and namely Tatianna—with my father.

The 1990s was a time of rebuilding for me. In 1990, I had been forty years old, and events had forced me to reinvent my life after opening and then selling a successful one-stop pet care business; opening a growing antiques shop; getting my MBA degree, which led me to a part-time teaching job at Northwood; falling in love with Ken; and losing him. With the exception of the antiques business, my teaching, and my darling Tatianna and Katarina, there was little left in my life from the 1980s.

The early part of the 1990s was a foggy and fuzzy time when I took each day as it came and worked through the loss of Ken and my father. In 1991, the university advertised a director of career services position, and I decided it was time to be out and about more, so I applied for and got the position. At the same time, I continued to teach a few courses a year. In 1994, Northwood launched a fast-track adult degree program, and they asked me to teach its first course, applied management. From that point on, my responsibility increased as I evaluated transcripts and work-life portfolios for college credit. I remembered the challenge it had been and commitment it had taken for Ken to juggle work, kids, school, and life and to complete his degree. That experience helped me to better connect with my students. Professionally, the future was encouraging.

The year after my father's death, my mother, sister, and I started a travel tradition. Every summer when I returned to the Midwest, we would set aside two to three days for us to go somewhere. The destinations reflected our interests—antiques, bed and breakfasts, gardens, and casinos. We had fun selecting different places to visit, making all of the plans, and actually going on the trip!

Personally, I was learning to adapt to a long-distance relationship with Joe. I found it challenging to go three to four weeks without seeing him. But he did his best to schedule time for us to get together in between his business trips. We made the most of holidays and three-day weekends. One summer, Joe surprised me with a trip to the Black Forest in Germany. While there, we visited a village where my seventh-generation ancestors had lived. Another year, he took me to London, my favorite city in the world. We also had many holiday dinners at The Breakers, one of the grandest hotels in the world, which was in Palm Beach near where I lived.

Although I had spent several years adapting to changes in my personal and professional life, another devastating change awaited me. One Sunday in mid-May 1994, I noticed that Marnie's sides were distended. She was having a difficult time lying down and could not seem to get comfortable. During a veterinary visit, the doctor extracted a lot of fluid to make her temporarily comfortable until they could diagnose the problem. Following several tests, we discovered she had a liver tumor. I was shocked because she had not been sick during the previous two years she lived indoors with me. She remained at the clinic through Wednesday. I visited her every evening, sat and held her, and told her how much I loved her.

On Thursday morning, Marnie had surgery to remove the tumor, but the veterinarian called me in the middle of surgery to deliver devastating news. The tumor had affected other organs, and he recommended putting her to sleep. I agreed. My beloved angel kitty exited my life as quickly and quietly as she had entered it. Much like my father's sudden passing, I had no time to prepare myself for her death. We had no time to say good-bye, and once again, I was reminded of the fragility of life. Indeed, she was a gift from God, and I wondered how I would ever repay this blessing. Tatianna and Katarina did not seem to be overly distraught by her sudden and untimely departure. We once again were back to a two-cat household.

When Can I Come In?
Marnie

CHAPTER TEN
TATIANNA BECOMES ILL

In my life's chain of events, nothing was accidental.
Everything happened according to an inner need.[1]
—Hannah Senesh

Tatianna had always been a healthy, vibrant cat. I had long envisioned her having the constitution to easily live fifteen to twenty years. Her routine veterinary visits included annual checkups, vaccinations, and teeth cleanings. Once, she had an infected paw, and she was troubled by an allergy usually in the spring. She was accustomed to spending time in the clinic kennel when I was away. She became good friends with Pat, the veterinary technician, and Bob, the animal groomer.

So when Tatianna became ill at age twelve, I was stunned. I took her to the clinic on Monday, June 17, 1998. Her behavior had changed in the preceding days. She was listless, vomiting, and drinking a lot of water. She went to her food bowl, looked at the food, but was unable to eat. And Tatianna loved to eat, so I knew there was a serious problem. The veterinarian drew blood samples and said the results would be available on Tuesday morning. Tatianna was a little dehydrated, so they administered some fluids, and then I took her home.

The next morning, Dr. Wright called me at work.

"You have a very sick kitty. You need to bring her to the clinic now."

I hurried home to get Tatianna. I took her back to the clinic, where she stayed until Saturday morning. I was devastated when I heard the diagnosis: acute kidney failure. Dr. Wright asked me about any household changes or any poisons that Tatianna may have ingested. I could not think of a single thing that could have affected her like this. The diagnostic work indicated a highly elevated BUN of 205 (with the normal range being 14 to 36). Her creatinine level was 11.3 (the normal range being .6–2.4). The BUN (blood urea nitrogen) and the creatinine tests were used to evaluate kidney function. She was in serious trouble. The elevated numbers indicated that urea nitrogen, a waste product of protein, was building up in the bloodstream rather than being cleared out. Tatianna was hooked up to an intravenous line and received a slow drip of many hundred milliliters of lactated fluids over the next several days.

I returned later Tuesday afternoon to visit her after she had gotten settled in and the doctor had ministered to her for the day. As I climbed the stairs to the surgical and kennel unit, I recalled the thousands of times I had gone up and down these steps when I was owner of Pet Apothecary. But that day was different. I was not assisting on a routine or emergency surgery. I was not there to feed the animals or walk the dogs. One of my own was there.

Tatianna was in a kennel at the end of the surgery room. This was a separate room from the usual boarders and other sick animals. It was also much quieter. Despite my thirteen years of veterinary experience, I was unprepared for what I saw. Tatianna was in the bottom kennel. An intravenous fluid bottle hung on the cage door, and the drip line was permanently taped to her front left leg. A slow drip of fluids was currently being given. Tatianna was very quiet and looked so unlike herself. She looked like her body had broken down tremendously in just a few hours. I dropped to my knees in front of the kennel and carefully opened the door. I began softly talking to her and stroking her.

"Oh, my sweet Tattie, I'm so sorry this has happened to you. I love you so much."

She responded with a deep moan, and I knew she understood me.

Dr. Wright came and explained to me what was happening.

"Tatianna's kidneys are not functioning properly, and toxins are building up in her body. This causes her not to eat or to vomit when she does try to eat or drink. She also tries to drink more water to help alleviate her problem. By giving her fluids, we are attempting to help flush out the toxins and ultimately bring down her blood work numbers. There could be severe and permanent damage with such elevated numbers. We will recheck the blood in a few days to determine what progress is being made."

I was devastated and could do little but cry. I went home alone and sat and held Katarina. She could sense that something was terribly wrong. Over the next few days, Katie cried a lot, too. She wandered aimlessly around the house looking for Tatianna. I wandered aimlessly myself. I prayed to God to help heal Tatianna and to keep her safe. Long, sleepless nights of despair stretched ahead of me. I prayed for morning to come quickly, so I could go visit her.

I returned to the clinic Wednesday morning. I sat on the floor with Tattie's cage door opened, and I talked to her and lightly brushed her.

"Oh, Tattie, it's so wonderful to see you. The house just is not the same without you there. Katie misses you so much. You are going to feel better day by day."

She looked straggly since she was not grooming herself because she was sick. She looked at me with that penetrating gaze, and we connected as kindred spirits. We shared the dimensions of love and pain with just one look.

The routine of visiting her every morning and afternoon continued. Then on Friday morning, they drew another blood sample to check on progress. The doctor promised to call me on Saturday morning to let me know the results. I slept very little Friday night because I was anxious about the future. I got up early so that I would be alert for the call. Several hours went by, and I did not hear anything. Finally, I could not wait any longer, and I called the clinic. The news was not encouraging.

"Although there has been a slight drop of the numbers, it was not what we had hoped. The BUN had come down to 158, and the creatinine rose slightly to 11.4 in about five days. Why not take her home for the weekend? She will probably be more comfortable in familiar surroundings and with her creature comforts," Dr. Wright said.

"Yes, I agree," I said.

"Do you want to try to administer fluids subcutaneously?" she asked.

"Whatever I need to do, I will," I responded.

Right before noon, Joe drove me to the clinic. I was upset, yet so glad Tatianna could come home—at least temporarily. I had no idea what the weekend would hold.

We went upstairs to the room where Tatianna had been hospitalized since Monday. Dr. Wright put her on the surgery table and removed the catheter for the IV. What happened next is an image indelibly etched in my mind and treasured in my heart. When the doctor finished the procedure, Tatianna rose up on her own accord and jumped into my arms. I embraced her. It felt so good to hold her close and feel the warmth of her fur. Gazing into her glistening blue eyes, I understood that the almost five-day separation had been just as excruciating for Tattie as it had for me. It was a blessed moment.

Joe drove us back home. Katie was so happy to see Tatianna. She rubbed and kissed her. I was mentally and physically exhausted. I had slept very little for days. So I placed Tatianna and Katarina in bed with me in the downstairs guest room, and we took an afternoon nap. Later in the afternoon, we went upstairs to the living room. I went outside in the backyard to get some fresh air.

Just a few moments later, Joe hollered at me, "Tatianna has just vomited!"

I was so frightened that I called Dr. Wright. She recommended that I increase the amount of fluids I was going to give Tatianna. We had been invited to a party that night, but I called and canceled. There was no way we were going to leave Tatianna alone on her first day back home.

Dr. Wright sent me home with a special prescription cat food called "k/d" and made by Hill's Pet Nutrition. Dr. Wright had explained that the nutritional formulation had reduced protein, phosphorus, sodium, and chloride, which would cause less buildup of the waste products that the kidneys normally removed. The food also had additives, such as B-complex vitamins. By feeding Tatianna the k/d food, we hoped to slow the disease's progression. During the years I worked in the veterinary business, I sold thousands of cans and bags of Hill's therapeutic food. I recalled the heartwarming beginning of Hill's business—a veterinarian formulated the first food for a guide dog with kidney failure after a blind man had asked the doctor to save his dog. That was in 1943. Here I was fifty-five years later, asking my doctor to do the same thing for my cat with kidney failure.

I mixed some water with the wet k/d food and put down a small plate. Tatianna ate voraciously. She had not been able to keep food down for over a week. I commented that she was starving. Later that evening, I had my first try at administering fluids to her. It did not go well. Tatianna was more than tired of being poked with needles from her stay in the clinic. I put her on a small round table in the middle of the kitchen. Joe held her down, and I attempted to insert the needle just under her skin on her right side. We suspended the drip set from a long metal plant hook placed over the top of the kitchen archway. The more Joe and I persisted, the more Tatianna resisted. We did manage to get some fluids into our unwilling patient. The second day, we discovered that the more lightly we held her, the easier it was.

When I was not in the same room with Tattie, I was crying. Joe spent the rest of the weekend trying to console and comfort me. I initially believed when I brought Tatianna home on Saturday that she would not make it through the next week. She had a serious disease, and it was more than likely that it had done irreparable damage. Joe canceled a business trip so that he could come back the following Friday to be with me.

However, after having cried for over a week, it suddenly dawned on me that all of this negative energy was a detriment to Tattie. Even though I tried to be cheerful around her, I knew she sensed how distraught I was. So I vowed to not think about a week from now and what events might unfold. Instead, I concentrated on the present moment exclusively. I promised I would be upbeat, happy, and hopeful. To be anything else would have been a disservice to Tatianna. I had used affirmations in my personal life to help boost my spirits, so on Monday, I decided Tatianna needed to hear an affirmation every day, especially when she had to have fluids. I hoped the power of good thoughts would help her. So I sat down and wrote the following affirmation:

> The spirit of faith shall heal the sick and
> God shall raise him up.
> The infinite healing presence is flowing
> through Tatianna as harmony and health.
> Tatianna is healed and whole.
> She is joyful, eating and drinking, and enjoying life
> with her loving companions, Katarina and Linda.
> Tatianna is healed, blessed, and restored.
> Through God, all things are possible.

During the first month of her illness, I repeated this affirmation six times a day. I repeated it at my office twice in the morning and twice in the afternoon. In the evening, Tatianna heard these words as I lovingly administered fluids to her.

All Dressed Up
Tatianna

CHAPTER ELEVEN
TATIANNA'S ACUPUNCTURE VISIT

What do we live for,
if not to make life less difficult
to each other?[1]
—George Eliot

I began learning everything I could about feline kidney disease. It is clinically referred to as *acute or chronic renal failure*. This common cause of illness and death in cats often occurs during the middle to senior years. Essentially, the kidneys filter toxins from the bloodstream, creating urine in the process. Often, without any apparent reason, the kidney function gradually declines to the point where the filtration rate is no longer adequate to maintain normal excretory functions. The toxins in the bloodstream begin to accumulate. When this happens, clinical signs such as excessive thirst, excessive urination, weight loss, lethargy, and vomiting are evident. Unfortunately, by the time these symptoms are evident, approximately seventy-five percent of the kidney function is generally gone. I learned that the choices for treating kidney disease in cats were limited. Dialysis was not an option, as in human medicine. Keeping the animal hydrated with fluids to flush out the kidneys was one of the main methods of treatment.[2]

I discussed with Dr. Wright alternative medicine options as well as the possibility of a kidney transplant.

She made several calls for me. Three veterinary schools in the nation did kidney transplants in 1998. The process included placing the cat on a waiting list until a donor kitty became available. Several weeks or months could elapse. In order to get a donor kidney, the cat had to sustain itself without fluid therapy (which made Tatianna ineligible) and be able to travel immediately once a donor was found. The cat was to remain in the hospital for approximately one month following the transplant. The recovery process could be difficult. After a successful operation, the cat and donor kitty (which the family agrees in advance to adopt) were to return home.

The next area I considered was Eastern medicine treatments. I learned that acupuncture and herbs could work together to rebalance the body system and to stabilize or to slow down the deterioration of body systems for certain medical ailments. At the time, a few veterinary schools offered a program in complementary and alternative medicine. We located a veterinarian in South Florida who specialized in acupuncture. Initially, we talked on the phone, and Dr. Pam Wood explained that she had success using acupuncture in both cats and dogs for a variety of ailments and diseases. One of her triumphs was treating kidney failure in cats. She indicated that some cats tolerate acupuncture, and some do not. Ideally, she would perform acupuncture during a series of three visits. Based on the cat's condition, she also recommended considering a change in diet and possibly herbal supplementation. She said she had had success with maintaining a good quality of life for a couple years with some of her feline patients. That was the most encouraging news I had heard in more than a week. She further explained that this approach worked in tandem with Western medicine, including fluid therapy and regular blood checkups. In other words, I was not choosing one practice over the other. So the two therapies would complement each other, with the two veterinarians consulting each other regularly. After speaking with Dr. Wood, finding out more about her credentials and training, and doing further research into Eastern medicine, I decided to take Tatianna to meet her.

The two of us set out on a forty-five-minute drive to Dr. Wood's office. Tatianna, who was always good in the car, was in her carrier in the passenger seat. The case was turned at an angle so she could see me. I could stick my fingers through the wire grating and touch her. I directed the air-conditioning vents on her to make her more comfortable.

I instantly liked Dr. Wood. I could sense she cared deeply about animals and their welfare. She asked me a lot of questions about Tatianna's medical history.

"How would you describe her health? Has she ever been seriously sick or injured? Is she on any medication now? How about in the past?"

I indicated that her health had been excellent. She had had an infected toe once from an ingrown nail. She also had suffered from an accidental burn on her back: Tatianna's food and water dishes were stationed under the microwave, and one morning as I lifted my teacup out of the oven, some scalding water had spilled onto her as she was eating. For a number of years, she had also had spring allergies. To relieve the incessant scratching, she had been prescribed a medicine called Ovaban.

She asked about Tatianna's sleeping preferences, too.

"Does she prefer to sleep under the covers or on top of the covers? Does she like to hide somewhere? Does she sit in the sun or hunt for a cool, dark area?"

Dr. Wood looked at Tatianna, examined her, smelled her, and listened to her heart and lungs. She was determining whether to classify Tatianna as "warm" or "cold," which, according to Chinese medicine, would dictate the kinds of foods and herbs that were best for her condition. Dr. Wood categorized her as "cold," which meant she should eat warming food that would help balance her cold condition. In Chinese medicine, foods have an affinity for different organs, and they can warm or cool us internally. To clarify, the food is not necessarily served warm, but as a result of being eaten, it generates internal warmth. Dr. Wood prescribed that Tatianna was to eat chicken livers, chicken, and egg whites to help her kidneys function better—and a daily herbal capsule that could be sprinkled on her food or poked down her throat. Her particular herb was an appetite stimulant. (A doctor could recommend other types of herbal medicines to restore blood flow, decrease toxins, and replenish potassium.)

Before she began the acupuncture treatment, Dr. Wood made a fuss over Tatianna.

"What a gorgeous cat you are!"

Tatianna responded positively.

The acupuncture went well. Dr. Wood inserted needles at different pressure points that correlated with the kidneys. A veterinary assistant held Tatianna in various positions; she cooperated without much of a tussle.

"Many cats do not tolerate the needles and go flying off the table. Tatianna is doing great," Dr. Wood said.

She also used a light meter machine and applied energy to several points, including Tatianna's legs. Then she returned Tatianna to her cage. I was very encouraged about how Tatianna had behaved. Dr. Wood sent me home with literature on acupuncture, dietary suggestions, and daily herb supplements. Dr. Wood also recommended I read the book *Four Paws, Five Directions—A Guide to Chinese Medicine for Cats and Dogs.*[2] I immediately ordered the book to give me a further understanding of Dr. Wood's approach.

I scheduled the next visit for two weeks later. A friend of mine drove us, and I held Tatianna's case in my lap. The second visit was uneventful. Once again, Tatianna rested on the table and allowed the acupuncture to be done. A third and last visit followed a couple weeks later, and another friend drove me. Dr. Wood said that we did not need to schedule any further acupuncture visits until after I had her blood checked a month later at Dr. Wright's office to determine how she was responding. They told me to continue with the daily fluid therapy, daily herbal treatment, and food therapy such as chicken and Hill's k/d prescription cat food.

By mid-July, a month following Tatianna's diagnosis, we had made major progress. Her BUN had dropped from a high of 205 to a low of 67. The creatinine had fallen from a high of 11.4 to a low of 5.7. Although the values were still out of the normal range, Tatianna was much improved. We were succeeding in stabilizing the disease!

Box Buddies
Tatianna and Katarina

CHAPTER TWELVE
TATIANNA'S DAILY RITUAL

**Where there is great love,
there are always miracles.**[1]
—Willa Cather

For almost three years, I decorated the archway of my kitchen with a suspended lactated ringers solution drip bag. I kept a box of needles in a kitchen drawer, and each day, I attached a new 22-gauge needle to the end of the drip line as the ritual began. Every day, I pulled the small, round breakfast table, which normally lived in the middle of the kitchen, over a couple feet toward the entryway so that it was within the reach of the drip bag. I always left a folded green terry cloth towel over the rungs of a high chair where a Raggedy Ann doll sat. It stayed there until I used it to cover the breakfast table after removing the white milk glass pedestal bowl, which held red papier-mâché cherries, and the embroidered towel under the bowl that read, "Life is just a bowl of cherries." It took two or three minutes to set the stage for the daily administering of Tatianna's fluids. Often she lounged in the dining room, and she intensively followed each of my movements with her relentless gaze, knowing that shortly I would pick her up and place her on the little round table. This daily ritual became our special time together and provided emotional and spiritual sustenance for us both.

When I lovingly gathered up Tatianna into my arms, I said, "It's time for your fluids, sweetie."

For both our sakes, we kept the ritual as lighthearted as possible. Tattie quickly learned the process, remarkably stayed on the table night after night, and accepted what was being done. Initially when I laid her on the table, she wanted to play for a few minutes. She grabbed the edge of the table and kneaded her paws back and forth, and then she sat up and looked at me or rubbed her head against me. As I talked to her in a calming voice and stroked her in a loving manner, she lay down and stretched herself out. We learned early on that this was the easiest way to place the needle under the skin subcutaneously and begin the fluid drip. She tolerated the needle, despite the fact that sometimes I had to stick her more than once. Sometimes, the needle came out if she moved suddenly. Infrequently, I hit a blood vessel accidentally, and Tatianna cried out, as a small stream of blood began to saturate her fur. Over the years, her skin became calloused, and it took two or three sticks before I found a spot that the needle could penetrate. But I learned how to use different parts of Tattie's sides in order to make it easier on her. Sometimes, I inserted the needle higher up on her back or closer to the front of her body. Other times, I found a lower point on the back that worked easier. Every once a while, Tatianna was just not in the mood for the ritual, the needle, and the dripping fluids, so she tussled with me. If she became upset, I just put the needle away for a while and walked away. Later, I scooped her up, and we were done with the fluid therapy before she knew it.

After the rigmarole of getting the fluids to begin to drip, I, without fail, recited the "through God, all things are possible" affirmation I had written for Tatianna. Sometimes, she closed her eyes, and other times, she gazed at me with her dazzling blue eyes. These were always moments when we felt deeply connected to each other.

After the affirmation, I began my soliloquy. Sometimes, I told her about my day—how hard or how easy it had been. If it was a day when I taught at Northwood University until 10:00 PM and did not get home until 10:30 PM, I tried to make up for being gone. Sometimes, I sang songs I had made up for her—like "Tattie is so sweet—she's so sweet, she's so sweet—Tattie is so sweet." Her eyes danced with merriment when I sang to her.

"I bet you have been in the sugie pills while I was gone," I teased.

As the last drops of fluids flowed into Tatianna, I ceremoniously recited the affirmation a second time.

Invariably, Katarina jumped up on the table during the half-hour ritual. Over time, she learned to be a part of it. She licked and kissed Tattie and made sure she was all right. Then she lay down next to her while I finished the fluids. I removed the drip line, draped it over the metal hook, and disposed of the needle. I left Tatianna on the table. Much of the time, she laid there indefinitely with Katie. Other times, she was ready to move on and hopped onto the red Lucy chair and then onto the tile floor. As she got older, I often helped her down, but she usually wanted to jump down alone. Once the two of them left the table, I undid the preparations and put the room back in order. I pulled the table to the center of the room, placed the green towel on the high chair rung, and returned the centerpiece to the table.

Without question, the time and loving attention spent in this daily ritual became Tatianna's lifeline and probably mine, too. The moment was reassuring and soothing for the two of us—and most of the time the three of us. It was as if, for that instant, all was well. We were together, and that was all that mattered. Our ritual became a sacred moment, providing hope and a positive energy flow. It strengthened our bond to one another as well as our connection to God.

By watching how Tatianna approached the daily needle sticking, I marveled at her quiet acceptance of the procedure coupled with her undaunted bravery. I told her constantly what a brave kitty she was to endure this day in and day out. It was as if she sensed that this was God's way of helping her to prevail in leading a quality life each day for as long as possible.

During the fluid therapy, Tatianna occasionally winked at me, a surprising and amusing habit she began when she was very young. I had always found myself wondering what special understanding she was sharing with me. Tatianna's wink had further added to her charm and joyous nature. What mysteries of the world did she comprehend? I could not even begin to fathom. However, without making a sound, I always sensed she was speaking with unquestionable insight to my soul.

Fluid therapy continued daily for most of the three years that Tatianna lived with kidney disease. I gave her from 100 to 200 milliliters a day depending on the stage of her condition. For a brief time during the middle year, we cut the fluid therapy back to every other day, which gave us some time off from the ritual, but I gave her higher dose at each treatment. However, I always repeated the positive affirmation to her twice a day whether or not she was getting fluids. We sat together in a chair, and I quietly repeated the affirmation. I believed in the power of the words and prayed that they could actually hold the illness at bay. I relentlessly sent positive reinforcement mentally in Tattie's direction anytime I was separated from her during vacations. I whispered the affirmation as I settled into bed surrounded by darkness. Although thousands of miles often separated us, I believed in my heart that Tattie could connect with my healing words.

The Daily Ritual
Tatianna and Katarina

CHAPTER THIRTEEN
TATIANNA'S TRIUMPHAL BATTLE

Normal day, let me be aware of the treasure you are.
Let me learn from you, love you, bless you before you depart.
Let me not pass you by in quest of some rare and perfect tomorrow.
Let me hold you while I may,
for it may not always be so.
One day I shall dig my nails into the earth,
or bury my face in the pillow,
or stretch myself taut,
or raise my hands to the sky
and want, more than the entire world, your return.[1]
—Mary Jean Iron

In the months following the kidney failure, Tatianna became stronger and stronger. Remarkably, all of us settled into the new routine that included daily fluids, herbal pills twice a day, food therapy, and affirmations. Although her appetite had increased, she ate small amounts of food at a time, so I fed her mini-meals throughout the day. I arranged my work schedule so I could come home more often for lunch. Her diet consisted of Hill's crunchy k/d and wet k/d, which I mixed with water to make a stew. She loved to lap this up. From Dr. Wood's recommended foods lists, I always had on hand fresh chicken livers or white chicken, which were big hits with Tatianna. I cooked the livers and then cut them into miniature pieces. Sometimes, I sprinkled them over the top of the k/d stew or fed them to her separately. I baked the chicken and cut it into very fine bits. My challenge was keeping the liver and chicken away from Katie. Invariably, she wrangled a couple morsels from me. Tattie also loved tuna. Although it was not on the dietary list, she got to enjoy it once in a while. We tried scrambled eggs, kidneys, and sardines, but they were not to her liking, so I took them off the recommended menu.

In the early months, we made frequent visits to Dr. Wright for updated blood work and weight checks. The diagnostic numbers improved dramatically! I kept a result chart for easy comparison from visit to visit. Every three months, I contacted Dr. Wood to get the herbal pills refilled. At one point, we switched to a Chinese herb called Eight Flavor Rehmannia. I gave her this small black pill twice a day to stabilize the failing kidney system and stimulate her appetite. Life was good for Tatianna. Clearly, a team effort contributed to God's blessing. Tatianna could not have done it alone, and I simply could not identify any one factor alone that made a difference. Our formula included nine facets: acupuncture, herbal pills, food therapy (the Chinese medicine menu and Hill's k/d prescription food), affirmations, fluid therapy, regular diagnostic work, a lot of love from Katarina and me, and an underlying spiritual connection. At that time, those factors complemented one another and had stabilized Tatianna's renal system. It took God, Dr. Wright, Dr. Wood, Katarina, and me. Everyone brought different assets—be it medical expertise, love, strength, bravery, faith, or an energy force—and all were necessary ingredients for our miracle.

Tattie began gaining back weight—from the lowest point of 11.8 pounds in August 1998 to her original weight of fifteen pounds by November 1999. Her lab work looked the best in March 1999 when her BUN was 65 and her creatinine was 4.6. The creatinine further dropped to 4.1 by October 1999.

Her impossibly blue eyes shimmered with life. Her coat grew shinier and silkier, and she resumed immaculately grooming herself and polishing her whiskers. She rearranged the multitude of term papers and assignments I had stacked around the house from the fifteen courses a year I taught at Northwood and crawled up in my lap whenever I sat down. I had learned to read a student marketing paper, hold Tatianna, and make comments on the paper simultaneously, because she simply had to be in my lap. She settled back into enjoying life with Katarina and me.

During Thanksgiving 1998, I lit a candle in celebration of Tattie's remarkable battle over the previous six-month period and prayed Psalms 75.1:

> We give thanks to thee, O God,
> we give thanks.
> We call on thy name and recount
> thy wondrous deeds.

I was truly grateful that she had lived life to the fullest as a thirteen-year-old. I thanked God for bestowing Tatianna on my life and for each precious moment that we had shared.

We learned to live with occasional water spit-ups. When her tummy was upset with toxins, she spat up, but generally, it was after drinking water. In January 1999, she began to crawl out of bed in the early morning, drink water from the bowl in the bedroom, and immediately vomit it up. It was almost as though when the cold fluid hit her tummy, it could not stay down. The doctors did not have any suggestions, and we learned to live with it. Sometimes, she went for days without spitting up, but it was impossible to predict.

Tattie and Katie's relationship continued to deepen. Their habits of sleeping and nesting together did not abate. As Tattie got stronger, their tussling games resumed to the merriment and amusement of all. They began to meet me in tandem at doors or the tops of stairs whenever I returned home. They pranced after me to the kitchen each morning for breakfast and followed me back upstairs while I got ready for work. Where one was, the other was not far behind. Their uncompromising devotion was, as always, a marvel.

In observing how Tatianna and Katarina interacted during their inseparable years together, I learned that, for them, the secret of life was simply about loving and caring for each other, day in and day out—nothing more, nothing less. They loved and cared for each other in fun, silly, and playful times and on ordinary days. This profound bond sustained them through the sad times of their relationship. The significance of this lesson struck me, and I knew God wanted me to comprehend and adopt it in my own life. God blessed my life with two awesome felines who delivered that message to me.

As I simply observed Tatianna during any of her antics and activities, I could not tell she had been near death and was living without proper kidney functions. There was a spring in her step, and she exuded a lighthearted spirit. Her carefree nature and playfulness amazed my family and friends. To me, she was a paragon of bravery.

The drip bottle, daily fluids, pills, specially prepared foods, affirmations, and trips to doctors—all became integral parts of our lives. Although there were many poignant and sometimes painful reminders that Tattie was coping with a serious disease, I did my best to focus on our present goodness in our lives.

But understandably, there were physical stabs of sorrow in anticipation of the future. The thought of someday losing Tattie overwhelmed me. I tormented myself by wondering, "Will it be next week? Next month? Six months from now? Will it be when I am on a trip or teaching a class? Will the ultimate surrender be unexpected or will there be guideposts along the journey?" The thoughts temporarily paralyzed me. Fortunately, I realized I could not live this way, and Tatianna would remind again to live in the present moment. I learned that animals are masters at focusing on the present moment. Tatianna enjoyed food when she was hungry. When Tatianna had her face in the food bowl, nothing else mattered. She appreciated the dappled sunlight and could lie for hours with its warmth enveloping her body. Light breezes that caught the lace curtains always captured her attention. Movements, such as a bird in the birdbath or a squirrel foraging for food, caused her to focus intently on the outside. When I arrived home, she focused on welcoming me properly. A kind word, a caress, or a scratch under the chin was special for her.

Tatianna was not enamored with the past and was certainly not focused on the future. She did not know she was not going to live forever, nor did she know all of the warning signs like I did. So she taught me that the present moment is truly all we can be sure of. I was grateful for each day that the three of us started together. I was grateful that Tatianna had an appetite, was involved in our household activities, played with Katie, and enjoyed lying in the morning sun. Once again, it was the present moment that mattered—not that she had become ill or that someday she would have to give up the battle. I refused to focus on the past or future thoughts. I could not change the past events and with God's help, I would deal with the future—when the time came.

So I enjoyed every moment for what it was. Several times a week, Tattie and Katie heard me say, "This is a special moment," or "This is a blessed moment." Simple, ordinary occurrences—Tatianna crawling in my lap, a wink from Tatianna, or Katie licking Tatianna while she got her fluids—precipitated these frequent comments.

Each month, quarter-year, half-year, and year became celebratory milestones. One month led to the next, and before we knew it, a year, two years, and then almost three years had passed. I thanked God for each additional day with Tatianna and for giving her a high quality of life.

We celebrated the ordinariness of days. On the surface, a quiet Sunday at home, when I slept in late and relaxed in the rocking chair with Tatianna draped over my lap, appeared to be ordinary. On the weekdays, listening for my car, which signaled my return to her world, and greeting me without fail was an everyday, ordinary occurrence. Likewise, we savored the daily activities of waking up, eating, drinking, and sleeping. We celebrated the holidays, and I went on vacation to Italy, Germany, and Great Britain. Tatianna and Katarina were boarding buddies as they had always been, and there was sweet jubilation each time we were reunited. Confronting and conquering medical odds were extraordinary accomplishments and gave us reasons to celebrate and give thanks every day. Tatianna reminded me that we were constantly surrounded by a myriad of blessed moments, most ordinary and a few extraordinary, that should never be taken for granted.

By 1999, I had many reasons to celebrate—my personal milestones, Tatianna's best year since she became ill, and the solid footing on which I had built my life. But there was one unresolved matter that led to another celebration.

As the calendar closed in on November 18, 1999, the ten-year anniversary of Ken's tragic death, it reminded me of how Ken and I had approached our relationship—day by day. Our relationship had mirrored the affection that Katarina and Tatianna shared. Over the past nine years as November got closer, I became increasingly agitated and restless. Sadness overwhelmed me. I wanted it to be different in 1999, but how to deal with the milestone baffled me. I entertained every notion from traveling to London for Thanksgiving to inviting Ken's sons and their families over to my yard to plant a tree. My soul implored me to not allow this moment to pass without serious reflection, because it was important for my growth and further understanding.

I fought the inner urge to reopen Ken's love letters—so long ago bundled up. I did not want to relive my pain, desolation, and hopelessness. However by witnessing Tatianna's relentless bravery in battling kidney failure, she inspired me to face the ghosts in the box of letters. So, in October 1999, I decided to read all of the love letters, cards, and notes Ken had ever sent me. The letters had been lovingly tied together and tucked away in the bottom of a big cardboard box. As I opened the outer box that housed Ken's personal papers, I removed a single red rose that had once been part of the casket spray. Tears immediately streamed down my face. "Maybe I cannot do this after all," I thought. But I kept on as I thought of Tatianna's courage. The box included his photo albums of our travels, a college transcript, grade reports, his high school diploma, old tax returns, an English essay, and photographs from a movie shoot. Then I quickly glanced at official papers relating to his death, such as hospital and insurance documents, estate papers, a death certificate, and a final tax return. In the wrongful death legal file was the deposition I gave, an autopsy report, homicide report, numerous letters from attorneys, and all of the final settlement papers. There was another file for my guardianship papers of Ken's younger son. Lastly, I found the personal representative estate file, which explained all I had to do to close the estate and settle the lawsuit.

But that day, I was not interested in poring over any of these documents or files. I unearthed the box for one reason. At the bottom of it were all of the love letters Ken and I ever wrote to each other. It had been years since I had explored this box teeming with sadness, loss, and, yes, love. As I uncovered the sacred stack of letters, I became still, and all I could hear was my pounding heart. I gently untied the blue ribbon. The hundreds of cards and letters took hours to read. I read every item Ken had ever given me, including the notes he had placed on my car's windshield. His letters wove together the threads of his devotion, caring, and thankfulness that made up our love. Then I turned my attention to all of the letters I had written him. Together, they chronicled our abbreviated but passionate relationship and illustrated our understanding of the good fortune we had had together. Holding the tear-stained letters that Ken had long ago penned to me epitomized how all encompassing and enduring his love for me is today and always. Just as Ken's love would always be a part of my life, I realized my fears of losing Tatianna's love someday were unfounded. She would always be tucked away in my heart.

God beautifies the seasons, creates fluttering butterflies, paints magnificent sunsets, flings stars into the universe, and never ceases to provide strength and hope in the midst of life and death. Upon reflection, I believe God granted Tatianna, Katarina, and me this stretch of time to savor the preciousness of our kinship, to learn new, life-altering lessons, and to say good-bye to one another. I knew there would never ever be another relationship quite like the one that the three of us shared. Interestingly, the interval between Tatianna's illness and demise was the happiest and saddest chapter of my life with Tatianna and Katarina. God gave us time to communicate and do all that needed to be done. There was no reason for regrets. Since Noelle, Taittinger, and Marnie had passed, I had learned to appreciate and embrace each moment for what it was.

In the same way, there would never be another relationship quite like the one Ken and I shared. I believed we were an unfinished love symphony. I always longed to say good-bye to Ken, and a lifetime together would have never been enough for us. However, I could take solace in the way we had daily loved and cared for each other. We recognized the gift God had given us and acknowledged our blessings often.

There is an old saying, "The past is history, the future is a mystery, and today is a gift. That is why they call it the present." Tatianna and Katarina were indeed gifts for me to enjoy each and every moment.

These Are the "A" Papers, Professor Mohr
Tatianna and Katarina

CHAPTER FOURTEEN
TATIANNA AND THE
CHRISTMAS CAT TREE

Not knowing when the dawn will come,
I open every door.[1]
—Emily Dickinson

Christmas in the Mohr household had always been a time of great celebration and activity. I wanted Tatianna's sixteenth Christmas to be the most special one she had ever had. Whether it was decorating trees, addressing cards, wrapping presents, or entertaining friends, Tatianna relished being in the midst of all of the festivities. She was the household's feline socialite. She loved to greet the company and was quite the charmer.

Tatianna also instinctively knew when guests who had not learned the joys of living with a cat entered the house. Then she took it upon herself to win them over. Instead of crawling into my welcoming lap, she landed in their laps or rubbed up against their legs. When they finally took a moment to notice her and really look into her eyes, she had them. She persisted until she captured their undivided attention. Inevitably, the guests commented on her extraordinary eyes, which truly drew you into the depths of her soul.

She particularly loved to lie under Christmas trees, and there were a lot of choices because decorated trees adorned every room of the house in 2000.

I was not always known as the "Christmas tree lady." In my young adult years, I simply decorated one live tree for the house as well as a tree for the pet business. Then one year, I decorated an artificial tabletop tree in peach ornaments and white pearls for the guest bedroom. A year or so later, I decided to do another tabletop tree, but this time I flocked it and adorned it with blue and silver ornaments. Another year, my sister wanted a violet-themed tree for her 1870 Victorian home Christmas tour, so I handmade ornaments and designed the tree down to the garland and lights. I liked it so much that the following year I made one for myself and one for the antiques shop. So my fascination with Christmas trees became a hobby where I designed and created trees to reflect the different rooms in my house.

Given my interest in antiques, I had an aluminum tree from the 1950s that I decorated with red and green balls and placed in the red cherry kitchen—but high on a ledge where the cats could not get to it. A vintage ornament and garland collection from the 1940s and 1950s hung on the tree in the master bedroom suite. The tree reminded me of the trees in my grandparents' home when I was a child. I used some of my father's baseball memorabilia to decorate the sports room tree. Red and white vintage Christmas cookie cutters dangled from a brass tree. A vintage bottlebrush tree collection covered the top of a breakfront. My collection simply centered on anything to do with trees and, of course, cat ornaments. (I also have my vintage Christmas tree brooch collection, which is one of my most prized collections—especially the pins that have cats climbing a tree or sleeping underneath a tree.)

Tatianna's favorite trees were the ten-foot live Scotch pine tree in the living room and the three-foot tabletop snow-flocked tree in the dining room.

During Christmas 2000, the live pine tree showcased exclusively more than two hundred cat ornaments—a collection that had evolved over Tatianna's lifetime. The Christmas cat ornament collection innocently started in 1982 while I attended a veterinary convention in Lake Buena Vista, Florida. I was shopping in a Christmas store and simply wanted to purchase a souvenir. Little did I know that the purchase of six porcelain cat heads, representing white, black, gray, calico, Siamese, and orange marmalade cats, would grow into a massive collection!

Unpacking and hanging the myriad of cat ornaments were rituals in and of themselves. The cat ornaments were wooden, metal, paper, hand quilted, glass, ceramic, plastic, resin, knitted, stainless steel, silver plated, hand painted, or felt. They were whimsical, angelic, simple, detailed, comical, or musical. Some had movable parts and jointed legs and arms. Collector ornaments included fragile Christopher Radco heirlooms, Garfield, Kliban, Gorham silver plate, Bradford Exchange, and Hallmark. Two exquisite Radco ornaments showcased two cats sleeping in blue snowflake mittens and a cat sleeping on beautiful packages. There were assorted cat colors represented, including gray, orange marmalade, white, black, tiger striped, tabby, and calico. The baubles depicted the cats in stockings, in trees, in garland, in holly, in wreaths, on skates, on pillows, in gifts, in trunks, in mailboxes, in carriages, in boxes, in boots, in baskets, in airplanes, with umbrellas, on picture frames, and on hymnals. They personified cats in dresses, in hats, with handbags, and holding parasols. They were baking, fishing, shopping, or snoozing. Cats wrapped themselves around candy canes or were decorated in lights and garland. Others peeked out of a Victorian shoe or popped out of a cat-in-the-box. Mice, fish, or red bells dangled from many ornaments.

I acquired the eclectic ornaments from friends, family, and my world travels. Some ornaments brought back tearful memories of Noelle and Taittinger. One reminded me of the year Noelle knocked over a seven-foot live tree while climbing to the top, and the tree had to be wired to a curtain rod for the rest of the season. Baby Taittinger especially liked to crawl under the tabletop tree decorated in peach and white and snooze for hours. Other ornaments reminded me of Ken. One in particular was a Hallmark ornament with a black cat and white cat playing peek-a-boo in a red plastic basket with a movable lid. A second white cat dangled on a string under the basket. If I pulled the string one way, the black cat's head popped out of the basket, and if I pulled again, the first white cat's head was visible. It was an amusing ornament and always made me laugh—just like Ken did. Another treasured ornament from Ken was two gray cats dressed as a bride and a groom.

I especially prized the Hallmark Keepsake Collection, because my mother has given one of them to me annually since 1985. The Hallmark cat ornaments were lighthearted and mischievous—just like Tatianna. One series of ornaments was called *Mischievous Kitten* and another *The Cat Nap*. My Hallmark collection spanned fifteen years, and the cats in it were up to a variety of antics, including hanging on a bird cage, laying over a fish bowl, wearing antlers, making cookies, sleeping in a knitting basket, climbing a Christmas tree, dangling from a stocking, and catching a bee on a poinsettia.

The ornaments from all over the world reminded me of my special travels. Some ornaments came from Macy's in New York; Harrods in London; the Black Forest in Germany; Paris; Rome; Savannah; San Francisco; as well as Frankenmuth, Michigan, a German-style village that boasts the world's largest Christmas store. But the ornament that had long ago captured my heart was a musical gray cat and marmalade cat together with a banner caption over their heads—"If I had but 9 lives I'd want to spend them all with you." It played "Let Me Call You Sweetheart." The ornament demanded a special spot on the tree; every year, I hung it at eye level in the middle of the front of the tree. The ornament truly epitomized Tatianna and Katarina.

Besides all of the cat ornaments, the tree included a wooden beaded cat garland, beanbag-style gray cats that mischievously climbed up into the top of the tree, a cat tree topper, and a cat tree skirt. An orange marmalade beanbag cat adorned in a red Santa hat was sleeping on a branch two feet from the top of the tree. Old-fashioned bubble lights and red bows completed the whimsical tree. It was indeed a tree with a lot of personality, not unlike Tatianna. For a month every year for sixteen Christmases, it was her favorite hideout. Standing near the tree was always a gray porcelain cat doll dressed in a Santa suit that bore a striking resemblance to Tatianna.

There were a multitude of moments to savor under a Christmas tree. First, Tatianna enjoyed batting at lower-hanging ornaments. She liked to watch their movement, and it entertained her to knock them onto the hardwood floor and bat them around the room. I learned over the years to hang paper, plastic, and tin ornaments at her level and reserve the fragile ornaments for the higher branches that were out of the reach of her furry little paws. This practice preserved the ornament collection! Another of Tatianna's favorite pastimes was to drink the water out of the tree stand, because it was always much more fun than walking to the water bowl in the kitchen. And after a long drink of water, she often decided to wedge herself between the brightly wrapped packages, enjoy the scent of pine, and snooze on the cat tree skirt. In the afternoon, dappled sunbeams filtered through the tree branches, warming Tatianna. She was totally content and stayed under the tree for hours. I took some of the most endearing photographs of Tatianna and Katarina in December 2000, as they slept together under the cat tree. It was a sight to behold; they were without question God's gift to each other—as well as to me.

The dining room Christmas tree sat on a square table between two wicker chairs. I decorated the heavily flocked tree with blue lights and silver, white, and blue ornaments to complete the icy, wintry look. A fluffy snow blanket enveloped the tree, and two blue-and-white porcelain cats and three crystal cats peeked out from under the blanket. Tatianna liked to go from one wicker chair to the other—not via the floor but over the table. She did not see a Christmas tree as a deterrent to this well-ingrained behavior. She climbed from one wicker chair to the tabletop; then she flattened herself, crawled under the tree, and jumped down into the wicker chair adjacent to the table. I could always detect when she had traveled this circuitous route, because the pieces of flocked snow on her fur gave her away. She looked like she had just come inside from walking in softly falling snow. Occasionally, she paused to lie under the tree, and her bluish gray-and-white coloring harmonized beautifully with the frosted winter wonderland tree. And if it was evening with the tree lights glowing, I could not help but catch my breath. Tatianna was beautiful. Remarkably, she never toppled over the tree, nor broke any ornaments!

I always had Christmas presents for Tatianna and Katarina. Their anxious little paws tore open soft, furry toys and edible treats. In 2000, their Christmas present actually arrived early in December, and I presented it to Tatianna and Katarina to enjoy beforehand. The red igloo bed was a wonderful safe haven with an opening of about six inches. The company designed it for one cat, and I had decided to try just one bed and see if either pet took to it. What a surprise—both Tatianna and Katarina adored the igloo and insisted in sleeping in it together! Another heartwarming picture was of them tightly and snugly packed into the igloo with only their little sleeping faces visible in the opening.

In my Christmas letter of 2000, there was, of course, a paragraph devoted to the felines: "On the furry front, Tatianna is now over fifteen years old, and she has been miraculously battling kidney disease for the past two and one-half years. We continue daily herbal and fluid therapy, k/d prescription food, affirmations, and occasional acupuncture. You would never know she was ill by looking at her. Katarina, now twelve, is her best buddy."

Silhouette Cats Under the Christmas Tree
Tatianna and Katarina

Waiting Patiently
Noelle

Which One's Mine?
Tatianna

Look Alikes
Tatianna and the Christmas Cat Doll

CHAPTER FIFTEEN
TATIANNA'S TRIUMPHAL
BATTLE WINDS DOWN

**Love is the only thing that we carry with us when we go,
and it makes the end so easy.**[1]
—Louisa May Alcott

My mother and brother visited us in Florida in mid-February 2001. I temporarily converted the sports room into a second bedroom to accommodate my guests. In the midst of all of the activities was Tatianna. She seized all opportunities to be where all of us were. She slept on my mother's bed, posed for my brother's camera, and curled up in any available lap. She was feeling great. I even saw her jump from my bed to the dresser—a feat that she had not tried for a long time. My mother was pleasantly surprised to see how healthy she looked and how interested she was in all of the household happenings. Her behavior reminded us of many years ago when she climbed onto the Trivial Pursuit board while my mother, father, and I were playing. She had loved being the center of attention as a kitten. Almost sixteen years later, the same was still true.

A month after my family's visit, Tatianna started her downward spiral. I had no warning that the last month of Tatianna's life would be the hardest for all of us, consisting of numerous visits to the veterinarian, diagnostic work, new medications, and even a blood transfusion.

Over the years, we had had our highs and lows. For example, in July 2000, routine blood work had shown slightly increased levels of BUN and creatinine compared to the fall of 1999. We had increased the amount of fluids, and Tatianna had started eating better. We were once again successfully managing the disease and riding on a high note. But this time, it was different. It all started quietly with routine blood work by Dr. Wright—a procedure we had followed since the onset of Tatianna's illness. The lab results revealed elevated phosphorus, and Dr. Wright gave us a prescription for PhosLo. This was the first time her phosphorus level had been out of the normal range since the onset of kidney failure almost three years ago. Then a few days later, Tatianna started vomiting up some blood, so we returned to see Dr. Wright. Tatianna was not acting herself. She was given 200 milliliters of fluids, Reglan for the vomiting, and an iron supplement. More diagnostic work showed a very low-packed cell volume of 12 which indicated anemia, and Dr. Wright recommended a blood transfusion. I discussed the options with Dr. Wood as well.

Decision time had arrived. Although we did not know whether the blood transfusion would provide the boost she needed, I decided we had to try it. Tatianna was cross-matched with a clinic cat and received a transfusion on March 21, 2001. After the procedure, I picked her up from the clinic in the afternoon and brought her home. Later that evening, she started bleeding on one side. I applied pressure to the area for most of the night to stop the bleeding and to ensure it did not start bleeding again. Tatianna perked up the next day as we had hoped.

After the blood transfusion, her treatment also included epogen injections three times a week to stimulate red blood cell production to fight the anemia. Meanwhile she was also taking medication to control her vomiting, as well as cimetidine tablets to help reduce the acid in her stomach. Her appetite had greatly diminished, so she was on cyproheptadine to stimulate her appetite. The doctor also gave her Nutri-Cal because she was not eating. Despite all the medications and blood transfusion, complications continued. Her back legs were beginning to swell, and she had labored breathing at times. Unfortunately, the epogen was not helping. She received epogen injections nine times between March 23 and April 13. But the packed cell volume only rose from the low of 12 to only 14, which was well below the normal range of 29 to 48.

One day, I would see some improvement, but then there would be a couple of hard days. Then there would be another good day or two when I thought we had beaten the odds for a while longer. One afternoon, as I waited in the veterinary examination room with Tatianna, she looked at me for a second with her twinkling eyes. I was taken aback. This spirited look had charmed me her whole life, and I had not seen that look in awhile. Could it be she had made the turn one more time? I went home with a spring in my step and sang to Tatianna and Katarina while I made chili. One Sunday morning shortly thereafter, Tatianna followed me to the kitchen, meowing and acting like she really wanted to eat. I knew she was hungry, but when I put the food down, she could not swallow it. I tried different items to no avail. (During that last month, my kitchen looked like a short-order diner. I had every possible kind of food that Tatianna had previously enjoyed—just in case something appealed to her.)

Katarina sensed her lifelong companion was in trouble. I started noticing that Katarina spent very little time with her. Tatianna had staked out a place to hide in the master suite—underneath a wooden antique file cabinet on legs in the office. I had recently reupholstered some dining room chairs, so I placed a large leftover rectangle of foam on the floor under the file cabinet and covered it with a fuzzy peach blanket. She loved curling up in this. I also placed a cardboard box at the end of the bed in case she wanted a step to jump onto the high bed.

Her interest in household happenings had subsided, and she rarely came downstairs. Her focus was on conserving energy in her safe, soft, dark, and quiet area, where she knew she would not be bothered. However, Katarina and I were close by, and we could see Tatianna from the bed. Many nights, I elected to sleep on the floor right next to Tattie, reminded of the days my vigilant Tatianna had stayed by my side while I mourned Ken's loss.

Katarina's behavior was more perplexing. Sometimes, when I carried her up to visit Tatianna, she would scamper off after a few minutes. They did not sleep together, and Katarina did not groom Tatianna. Finally many weeks later, I understood Katarina's behavior. I realized they had said their good-byes and were getting used to being alone. I think they sensed and accepted the end long before I did.

I read somewhere that what cats do best is cope. Tatianna certainly did. I do not think cats worry like human beings do. If they are fed late, they cope by opening doors or knocking over trash. If the house is cold, they instinctively look for sunbeams, crawl up on a warm, upholstered chair, or burrow into a comforter. If they are too warm, a glass-topped table or tile shower stall is comforting. They do not worry about what will happen tomorrow or when the miracle cure will help them. They live for the moment.

Yes, cats cope—and Tatianna was no exception. Throughout her life, she coped with my schedule. She waited for me to return home, waited to be picked up from boarding, waited to be fed, and waited for me to wake up in the morning. To me, the most interesting coping mechanism was her instinct to conserve energy by hiding out when she struggled at the end.

I had looked forward to the Good Friday holiday as a welcomed day off from work, filled with sleeping late and spending precious time with Tatianna and Katarina. But the day turned out to be anything but good. Tatianna was weak and listless when I awoke. I called the clinic and immediately took her to see Dr. Wright. She had diminished eye-reflex action when I tapped near her eyes, and I knew from years of working with animals that that was not a good sign. I remembered how the night before, she had winked at me during the fluid ritual, and her current condition reminded me of how quickly life could change. Once again, they drew blood samples for analysis. The results would be back the next morning.

We returned home. I discovered Tatianna could no longer jump onto her favorite living room chair. I helped her up, and she rested there for a while. Later, I moved her to a box turned on its side on the dining room floor where she could feel more secure. That night, she crawled out of the box to where I was sitting and kneaded her paws on the top of my shoes. I was astounded. She barely had the strength to move, and she was engaging in her endearing, trademark gesture. I reached down and caressed her.

"Oh, Tattie, you have no idea what this means to me. You never cease to amaze me with your relentless love."

That day challenged us. Tatianna and I remained in the living and dining area. I tried to read while keeping my eye on Tatianna. Katarina disappeared, as she had done most of the previous month. I left the house briefly to run an errand, not yet fully comprehending that the end was so near. If I had known, I would have stayed home.

In the early evening, I moved Tattie from the dining room into the living room, placing her gently on the twelve-by-sixteen-inch box she had lovingly adopted a year ago after I had emptied its contents. The box resided under the Queen Anne coffee table. It was big enough for her to stretch out, and she could exercise her front paws by rubbing on its well-defined edge. Sometimes, she stretched out and slept on the box for hours. That day, she lay there for a while and then tried to get up. But she did not have the strength to do so. I was going to help her up, but before I could reach her, she let out a banshee cry unlike anything I had ever heard.

"My dear, sweet Tatianna, what's wrong? Do not worry, I will keep you safe."

But I was getting more and more worried by the moment. I decided to go ahead with the evening routine of giving fluids and medications.

I placed Tattie on the little kitchen table, where she had been hundreds of times. I repeated the precious affirmation that I had said more than two thousand times and stroked her tired body. Katie, playing her supporting role flawlessly, appeared from hiding and jumped up to lay next to her. After I finished the fluid therapy, I stepped away from the table, leaving Tatianna and Katarina. Often, they rested together for an hour or so. But that evening, Tattie attempted to get off of the table while I had left the room. When I returned a few minutes later, she was flat on the floor, and I knew she had fallen hard when she tried to jump off by herself. I scooped her up in my safe arms and held her tightly against my heart.

Tatianna and I spent the rest of the evening in the living room. I reflected on the day, starting with the unanticipated trip to the veterinarian's office due to

Tatianna's listless, lifeless manner. Then in the midst of the predictable behavior of Tatianna's normal kneading of my shoes was the uncharacteristic behavior of the banshee cry. Then came the realization that Tatianna could no longer jump up and down from her favorite living room chair, which was followed by her falling off of the kitchen table. I flipped through some magazines while I watched Tatianna. Occasionally, I picked her up and put her in my lap, but she was more comfortable on her box. Katarina darted in and out of the living room and ignored us.

Later that evening, I put her back on the table to force-feed her. I got a few drops of Nutri-Cal down her. She was not resisting, but I knew she did not like what I was doing. Throughout the past month, I had asked her to give me a sign when enough was enough and we needed to say good-bye. So when she looked up at me with those soul-stirring eyes and put her right paw up to block the next syringe of food, I knew she had given me that sign. Over fifteen years ago, I had mistakenly prolonged Noelle's life. I would not make the same mistake with Tatianna. Once again Tatianna's nonverbal communication spoke volumes to me. I knew she was telling me, "No more. Let's stop this now. It's time to end it." I immediately honored her request and put down the syringe. A single tear glittered on my right cheek as Tatianna lowered her head in graceful acceptance.

I lovingly gathered her up in my arms again and carried her up to the master suite. I put her on the little foam mattress with the fuzzy peach blanket where she'd been used to staying for the past month. As I got ready for bed, Tatianna staggered off of her spot and attempted to make her way to the litter box in the bathroom. I could not believe her determination. I gathered her up and carried her to her destination. She was so tired and depressed. But I had not realized that the end was so near, that she had let go. I had not realized I had witnessed her last wink or the last kneading of my shoes. I had not realized we had spent the last evening together in the living room. I had not realized that I had administered fluids to her for the last time. Unlike Katarina, I had not realized I would never see my precious Tatianna and Katarina on the kitchen table again, caring for one another.

Around midnight, we settled down together at the end of the bedroom for the last time. She purred as I stroked her body.

You're the best!
Tatianna and Katarina

CHAPTER SIXTEEN
TATIANNA'S LAST
MORNING

This has reached its proper perfection.
This has become what it has in it to be.
Therefore, of course, it would not be prolonged.
As if God said, "Good, you have mastered that exercise.
I am very pleased with it.
And now you are ready to go on to the next."[1]
—C. S. Lewis

That day was the day—the day I had played out in my mind for years. That day's main drama proved to be my ultimate test in unselfish love. Even when Tattie was a kitten, my eyes welled up with tears just thinking when she would no longer be by my side. During her illness, I found myself imagining what it was going to be like at the end, and I ended up crying uncontrollably.

I awoke around 3:00 AM to check on Tatianna. She had crawled off the blanket onto the bare floor. I put her into the litter box that I had moved closer to her a few hours earlier. She could not hold herself up. I lifted her out of the litter pan and sat down on the floor beside her. After a while, I moved her to the end of my bed. I lay next to her and held her front paws with my right hand. We slept like that until 7:00 AM.

On the surface, the day started out much like any other April Saturday morning in my household. The sprinklers started watering the grass around 4:00 AM. The pool pump switched on at 8:00 AM. The sun shone in the living room's picture window where Tattie, Katie, and I would normally have been stationed for a relaxing morning. The temperature was seventy degrees and would reach a high of nearly eighty degrees. The weather would be glorious today. It was an everyday, ordinary day in South Florida.

Is that not the irony of life and death? We live everyday, ordinary days until it is time to go, and then one day, we die on an everyday, ordinary day. But the house continues with its schedule and Mother Nature continues with her plans.

When I saw her at 7:00 AM, I knew this was the day. I flashed back to just a few hours before, when Tattie had raised her paw to stop me from force feeding her. In her way, she had said that it was okay to surrender after the good fight we had waged, and I had to accept that this was the end and that her life had come full circle. She had fought valiantly and gracefully, and in return God had blessed her with a high-quality life for almost three years after being diagnosed with kidney failure. We had done all we could do, and there would be absolutely no regrets. Tatianna was not going to get stronger; she could no longer rebound. But that was all right. My dear, sweet, indefatigable Tatianna was now lifeless and profoundly exhausted. I could feel the very essence of life being pulled out of her being. Her extraordinary, light-spilling blue eyes were now dead, glazed over, and totally unresponsive when I tapped above them. She simply stared straight ahead. Nothing held her attention here anymore. She was truly off in another realm even though her body was still lying on the bed. It seemed to me she had gone into another dimension in an eye blink. Perhaps, this was God's way of gracing our lives. When the end came, it would just be there, quickly and swiftly. It would not be long and drawn out for both our sakes. Just a week ago, she had staged a mild rally by walking into the kitchen, looking for food, but that day, a heavy pall of desolation settled over me and cut to the innermost core of my being. Watching my beloved Tatianna deteriorate so suddenly was heartbreaking. Another beloved friend was about to complete the circle of life. Noelle, Taittinger, Ken, my father, and Marnie had all entered in my circle and departed. That day, it was Tatianna's turn, and we would get through it. Tatianna had masterfully taught me that difficult battles can be endured through bravery, strength, faith, and love.

Dr. Wright was supposed to call me in midmorning with Friday's blood results to try to determine why Tatianna was not eating. Ironically, it poignantly reminded me that almost three years ago on a Saturday morning, I waited nervously by the phone for the results of Tatianna's blood work after she had been hospitalized. I knew when she called this time, I would have to ask her to put Tatianna to sleep. It was time for me to say good-bye and send her back to God with honor and dignity. I knew the clinic closed at 1:00 PM. I began counting the hours left before the clinic closed. I petted her and talked softly to her.

"I love you, Tattie. You have been the best gray cat ever. It is all right to let go now, my dear Sweetie Tweetie."

There were barely any movements from her—no tail swishing back and forth, no eye movement. It was heart wrenching to watch.

I was extremely restless. I threw on a blue denim jumper appliquéd with pink and blue kittens. My hair was a mess, but I did not care. I combed it back the best I could and put on some pink lipstick. Then I returned to Tattie's side. But I could not sit still, so I headed back to the kitchen. Her potassium supplement and Nutri-Cal were on the counter as well as two kinds of antacid medicine. I scooped them up and threw them in the trash, because I unequivocally knew that she no longer needed them.

I ran back up the stairs to Tattie and resumed the talking softly to her and caressing her. It was 10:00 AM. The morning was passing by with lightning speed. I began playing a game with myself. "If Dr. Wright does not call in the next half hour, I will call to the office," I thought. I certainly did not want there to be any miscommunication. I did not want to miss her, in case she had plans to leave the office earlier than usual this Easter weekend. She did not call. I extended the game and waited another fifteen minutes before I realized that Tatianna's last hours were on the brink of Easter morning—another loss incurred on a holiday. I called, and Bob answered.

"Bob, this is Linda Mohr. Is Dr. Wright available?"

"She's with a client right now, but I will have her call you just as soon as she's done," Bob said.

About half an hour later, she called and immediately started giving me the results before I could say anything.

"We just got the blood results, and they look pretty good. The BUN was 116 and the creatinine was 7.6. The phosphorus/calcium/potassium levels were in the normal range. Tatianna will not need the potassium supplement anymore."

I listened quietly as Dr. Wright conveyed this encouraging information from her report. However, I had to tell her about Tattie's condition in the last twelve hours.

"Dr. Wright, Tattie has quickly gone downhill since last night. She let out a banshee cry the night before and put her paw up to stop me force-feeding her."

She listened quietly as I forced out the strangled words to recount the details of the previous day.

"Would you kindly come to my house and put Tatianna to sleep?" I heard myself say.

"Certainly I will."

She then put Pat on the phone for the specific arrangements. It was now 11:15 AM. We had an hour and fifteen minutes left before they were planning to arrive.

I hung up the phone, returned to the bedroom, and sat on a bench at the end of the bed. Tattie had not stirred at all. I continued to talk softly to her and stroked her. I knew it was time to read her the Rainbow Bridge poem, a beautiful poem I had found in one of my books—*Angel Whiskers ... Reflections on Loving and Losing a Feline Companion.*[2]

"Sweetie, help is on the way. I have a special poem to read to you."

> There is a bridge connecting heaven and earth.
> It is called the Rainbow Bridge because of its many colors.
> Just this side of the Rainbow Bridge,
> There is a land of meadows, hills and valleys with lush green grass.
> When a beloved pet dies, the pet goes to this special place.
> There is always food and water and warm spring weather.
> The old and frail animals are young again.
> They play all day with one another.
> There is only one thing missing.
> They are not with their special person who loved them on Earth.
> So each day they run and play until the day comes
> When one suddenly stops playing and looks up!
> The nose twitches! The ears are up!
> The eyes are staring! And this one suddenly runs from the group!
> You have been seen, and when you and your special friend meet,
> You take him or her into your arms and embrace.
> Your face is kissed again and again and again,
> And you look once more into the eyes of your trusting pet.
> Then you cross the Rainbow Bridge together, never again to be separated.

After I finished reading the poem, I added a line: "And it will be a glorious reunion." I continued to speak reassuringly to her, because I believed she could hear me even as she slipped into another realm.

"I am not upset that you have to tell me good-bye now. I will be fine, and I will always love and adore Katie—just like you did."

For a minute, I was unbelievably calm, and I kept telling myself to breathe. I simply asked God to just get me through the next fifteen minutes, then the next, and the next. But then I could not stand it another minute, and I ran down to the third level of my house with some of Tatianna's bedding. I broke into uncontrollable sobs as I leaned against the laundry room wall and remembered how many years ago I had rescued Tatianna from the clothes dryer caper. Oh my, what living we had sandwiched from that day in 1985 to this morning in 2001! As I reminiscedd, I calmed down. Then I ran back upstairs to check on Tatianna.

I decided to move her from the bedroom down to the small kitchen table where she had received her life-sustaining fluid therapy and affirmations and where she had been helped, loved, and restored for almost three years. It seemed the perfect location for the end of her life. I gathered her up and buried her lovingly in the circle of my arms as I had done a myriad of times over her lifetime. My arms had been a safe haven for her, and she had loved to be held this way. I slowly walked down the stairs to the second level into the kitchen. I wanted to savor every moment as I cocooned her close to me. I knew that was the last time I would take this walk with her and hold her like this.

"Tattie, your doctor and Pat will be here soon," I told her before I began singing, "you're so sweet, you're so sweet, sweet Tatianna."

I wondered how many thousands of times she had heard that sound in her earthly journey and whether she could hear me now. I believed that she could. Then I kidded her one last time.

"I bet you have been getting into the sugie pills when I was not looking."

Her extraordinary sparkling eyes gazing at me were now poignant memories emblazoned in my soul. She was calm and peaceful. I was remarkably calm and peaceful, too. We had abandoned the struggle. In its place, God blessed with us serenity. The silence and a sense of incredible calm surrounded us.

There was a tap at the front door. I knew who had arrived. I bent down and kissed Tatianna on the top of her head.

"I love you, Tatianna, always and forever. Someday I will see you on the Rainbow Bridge, and it will be a glorious reunion."

I will always remember this poignant and personal good-bye.

When I opened the door to greet Dr. Wright and Pat, the words stuck in my throat and nothing came out. If I could have reached down into my throat, I would have found words—or more likely, my heart. It was the first time in my life that I had experienced anything like that. I held the door open for them and managed to usher them into the house. I could read their questioning faces, because they did not see Tatianna in the living room, but I still could not speak. I led them into the kitchen. I finally managed to caution them as they followed me.

"Please watch your step, as the floor slopes from the dining room into the kitchen."

I turned on the bright overhead track lights and a fanlight that was hanging just over the little table.

"Thank you so much for coming."

"Has Tatianna been like this since early this morning?" Dr. Wright asked.

"Yes," I said.

"It is the anemia."

They both petted her, and Dr. Wright bent down to her.

"This just is not like you, is it?"

Indeed, Tatianna, who had charmed and delighted all who met her, who had pranced jauntily around the house, and who had loved and adored Katarina, was not anything like this. Dr. Wright took a paper and pen out of her briefcase.

"Do you want a general or private cremation?"

"Private," I softly responded.

She checked off the boxes for euthanasia and private cremation. I signed my name by both and also signed at the bottom.

"I guess I did not need to sign everywhere," I mumbled.

I blew my nose on a Kleenex that I had stuffed in my jumper pocket.

"I hope she has not been suffering long."

No one said anything else. What could one have possibly said? What could I have said that I had not said a thousand times? We had lived our time together in total devotion and love. No words could properly convey my feelings at that time. The moment was very quiet, and a reservoir of other-worldly calm hovered over the four of us. I knew we were not alone.

The doctor broke the silence.

"Are you ready? We are."

"Yes," I softly replied.

Then I bent down and stroked Tattie on the right side. Her head was facing me. Dr. Wright tapped a vein on Tattie's left paw that had previously been shaved for the transfusion. She took a drip needle out of her bag. My hand touched Pat's hand. I remained composed. I saw Tatianna's breathing stop, and I knew she was now safe and whole.

Dr. Wright's stethoscope confirmed, "She's gone."

Like a switch being flipped, the brightness of life had gone out of Tatianna. Tatianna, who had provided me with perennial joy, was now in God's safe harbor. I reached over and closed her once-mesmerizing eyes that had benevolently allowed me into her soul for almost sixteen years. I silently prayed that I would always remember her eyes.

"Let them always be a still frame in my mind."

The three of us stood there reverently. Then Pat smoothed out the towels that Tattie was lying on.

"What would you like to take Tattie away in?" I asked.

"I have a bag," she said.

I had not noticed it, but Pat removed it from the back of a kitchen chair. She opened the bag and, with the help of Dr. Wright, lowered Tatianna into it. Tatianna's body was still warm but limp. That limpness was not my glorious Tatianna.

Pat hugged me and said, "I am so sorry."

"Thank you for all of the years that you have cared for Tatianna."

I hugged Dr. Wright.

"Thank you for coming to the house. We just could not make the final drive to the clinic," I said.

I showed them to the door. As they descended the nine front steps to the driveway, I remembered when I had carried Tatianna as a kitten down the neighbor's steps and brought her safely home after her outdoor escape. More than fifteen years later, Pat carried Tatianna down our home's steps to return her safely to God's house. I watched until Pat and the black bag holding Tatianna were out of sight. Then I wept.

Sometimes, the anticipation is worse than reality; sometimes, it is not.

CHAPTER SEVENTEEN
THE HOURS AFTER

**You gain strength, courage, and confidence
by every experience in which you really stop to look fear in the face.
You must do the thing which you think you cannot do.**[1]
—Eleanor Roosevelt

I collapsed in complete exhaustion after Dr. Wright and Pat departed. I headed straight to my bed. On the way upstairs, I poked my head into the violet room, where Katie was sleeping in a wicker chair. She had made herself scarce throughout the morning drama. After about half an hour, the phone rang, and something prompted me to make the effort to answer the call. It was Joe. He could tell by the way I said hello that something was wrong.

"I just had Tatianna put to sleep about an hour ago," I sobbed.

He lovingly expressed his condolences and then said that he had been out running errands, and the notion suddenly overtook him to call me.

As the afternoon wore on, Katie became more and more agitated. She crawled up on the bed and sniffed the area where Tattie had spent the last few hours of her life. Then she poked her nose down between the mattress and headboard. She jumped off of the bed and proceeded to look in open closets. She searched the office area at the end of the master suite. She wandered from room to room, hunting for her beloved companion. Her actions reminded me of how Tatianna had searched for Taittinger after Taittinger's passing almost fourteen years ago. My heart was breaking for Katie. The long and glorious reign of Tatianna and Katarina had ended. Just like the moment when Ken's doctor told me my life would never be the same after his passing, I knew this was one of those life-altering events. My life would never be the same without the two of them eagerly waiting to welcome me home every day. Katarina's life would never be same without her precious friend. I drifted in and out of a semiconscious state. Once, I thought I felt paws walking on the bed, and I knew Tatianna's spirit still lingered in the house.

I was much like Katie—restless and beside myself. I could not lie down or sleep. I was unable to concentrate on anything for more than a few minutes. I went to the kitchen, took down the fluid bag that had been a permanent fixture for almost three years, and threw it in the trash. I removed the towels from the kitchen table, which had long grown cold from the last warmth of Tatianna. I put them in the washer. I removed the cardboard boxes from the living room and dining room and threw them out onto the patio. Later, I brought one of them back to her designated spot, because I was not ready to discard it.

I cried, and I rocked. I tried to read, and I held Katie. I was simply numb and exhausted. An unbearable ache of loneliness clothed my heart. Later in the evening, I called my mother, who I knew could understand what I was going through, because she had lost her beloved twelve-year-old cat to kidney failure in 1996. She was devastated to hear the sad news. She said Tatianna had had the best possible home for a very long time, and she was right. Joe called me again late that night. I was afraid to go to bed because I did not want to have nightmares. At midnight, I forced myself to try to go to sleep. Katie immediately joined me and started licking away the uncontrollable tears that were streaming down my face. I fell asleep until 4:00 AM and tossed and turned for quite a while. I relived every moment of the previous twenty-four hours. I finally drifted off to sleep until 7:30 AM. When I awoke, I simply could not move. I tried to get up, but my legs did not cooperate. I collapsed back into the featherbed and just stayed there, contemplating what was waiting for me. Once again, the ordinariness of the day struck me. Soft sunlight filtered through the wooden shutters in my bedroom. Birds chirped in the pink grapefruit tree just outside the window. I heard a jogger pass the house. The neighbors were enjoying their Sunday morning coffee on the patio. But I was afraid to get up. I was afraid to go to the kitchen. I knew I would be listening for Katarina and Tatianna's paws padding behind me as I made my pilgrimage to the kitchen. In reality, Katie would be the only one following me, and this would be the first Sunday from now on that I would not spend part of it with Tatianna.

I managed to will myself out of bed around 10:00 AM. I fed Katie, made tea, and opened the windows. I opened the front door and looked out the screen door. Something had pulled out the plant in a tall metal container out front, and it lay on the brick landing. When I peered out the back door, something had moved the box that I had put there the previous night. Were those things signs that Tattie had been there? Was this her way of telling me she was fine? Joe called me at 11:00 AM to check on me. I spent the rest of the day in my rocking chair, and sometime that afternoon, I penned the outline for Tatianna's book.

I could feel Tatianna's spirit, which had embraced the entire house, everywhere. Today was no different. I could not escape by moving to another room. Her favorite spots were everywhere. I could not simply close off a room to make it a shrine. The only escape for me was outside, because that had not been part of Tatianna's world. But was it now? Was it not possible that her spirit encompassed the universe?

That night, there was no ritual of fluids, herbal pills, or forced feeding. There was no cradling her in my arms as I carried her to her sleeping quarters. There was no need to lie on the floor with her and check on her every few hours. I was lost and desolate.

Before I went to bed, I added a list of my poignant memories to the book outline that exemplified Tatianna's personality. Invariably, as I pored over these memories, they included Katarina, too. How could I forget Tatianna's loving Katarina and running to Katarina if she cried? How could I forget the two of them greeting me at the top of the stairs when I returned home? Oh, to see them this way just one more time!

Tatianna was notorious for shredding toilet paper, adopting cardboard boxes as her furniture, getting on the bed as I changed the sheets, playing musical chairs with me, playing peek-a-boo behind the shower curtain, and watching me from a window when I was outside. Oh, to see just one of these antics one more time!

I could find Tatianna sleeping in the baby buggy, on the featherbed, in the picture window, in a spoon-like position with Katarina, under the cat Christmas tree, in the red igloo bed on her last Christmas with Katarina, or in her favorite spot, my lap. Oh, to find Tatianna sleeping anywhere just one more time!

Of course, I recalled her signature move—kneading her paws on the top of my shoes whenever I sat down. The most crystal-clear memory was her eyes, which had been her defining and endearing characteristic. I would always remember her winking at me, socializing with and charming my company with a simple look, lying in a chair and following my every movement with her eyes, gazing up at me and wanting to be in my lap, and connecting with me simply by looking into my eyes. Oh, to look down at my feet just one more time and see Tatianna's magical eyes!

Finally, I recalled what it was like to be reunited with her after a long journey. Oh, to hug her just one more time!

Of course, it was impossible for this myriad of memories to be reenacted other than in my mind. Remarkably, merely revisiting Tatianna this way had a momentarily calming effect on me. Tatianna had been a true treasure. I prayed that I would always be able to open Tatianna's treasure chest and recall her in vivid recollection as I had done that evening.

I retired around midnight, and Katie heard me crying in bed. She once again licked away my tears. I was awestruck that Tattie, through taking care of Katie, had taught Katie exactly how to take care of me. Tattie had taught her well, and in my heart, I knew we were going to get through this. Katie was restless and came and went throughout the night. I awakened again around 4:00 AM, and my first thought was "Tatianna is dead." I started wailing, and Katie immediately appeared and kissed my face.

I flashed back to more than fifteen years ago and saw my little gray kitten, snuggling next to my beautiful orange marmalade cat, Noelle, who was dying of cancer. Even though Noelle had been the queen of my household for ten years, she had surprisingly welcomed Tatianna into our world. The night after Tatianna's death, I clearly understood why Tatianna had arrived on the twilight of Noelle's life. Noelle had important lessons to teach that little ball of gray fur.

I also had lessons to learn from Noelle, but I just had not recognized it. So in retrospect, Noelle had shown me that love was never-ending, and we were all connected. I had been devoted to Noelle and mistakenly had thought there was no more room in my heart for another kitty. But in reality, my heart expanded to fill the love available to me. Noelle had shown me that she could embrace, accept, and love the little gray kitty because she was now part of our family. She had wanted me to see that Tatianna would be around long after she had to leave and that we would love and care for one another. Yet, we also would eternally be a part of Noelle's circle of life and continue to impact each other in incredible ways.

"Thank you, my master teacher, Noelle. I finally got the message," I whispered with gratitude.

The Peek-A-Boo Lilacs
Katarina

CHAPTER EIGHTEEN
TATIANNA'S JOURNEY
WITH LINDA

**The soul should always stand ajar,
ready to welcome the ecstatic experience.**[1]
—Emily Dickinson

I spoke with my dear friend Nikki a day before going on a four-day business trip from Florida to Michigan. This trip was just ten days after Tatianna's death, and I was not looking forward to leaving town so soon. Fatigue paralyzed me, and boarding Katie by herself for the first time concerned me.

After sharing those thoughts with my wise friend, she asked, "Why not take Tatianna with you?"

I did not know what in the world she had meant. She went on to explain she often took her mother, father, or even Rascal, her dog, with her in spirit, depending on the circumstances or challenges she had to face. She told me I could then draw on Tatianna's strength, and my business presentation would be powerful. The notion intrigued me, and I thought, "How ironic."

For more than fifteen and one-half years, I had typically traveled a month for vacation and generally to a couple of conventions or business trips a year. Tatianna never got to go with me—she always spent the time in the boarding kennel. But now, was it possible that she could see what I often did when I had left her for extended periods of time? In fact, I would not even have to go on an out-of-town journey—Tatianna could accompany me any time and any place in her spiritual form!

Traditionally, I enjoyed draping her over my back and left shoulder and carrying her around the house to entertain her. So, I decided my shoulder would be her spot on our special spiritual missions together. But this time around, she would be facing forward, so I would be able to reach across with my right hand and pat her on the top of the head and pet her front paws. I would also be able to rub the side of my face against hers. I wanted her to see where we were going, not where we had been. We had grand adventures ahead of us.

My friend also gently suggested to me that it might be a healthy change of environment for Katie and me to be out of the house and away from the raw, painful memories for a few days. If taking Tatianna with me in spirit helped soothe my hurt, then why not? What harm could it possibly do if it did not work? So I agreed with Nikki, whom I considered to be a highly evolved spiritual being with an uncanny sense of understanding the unexplainable. I felt especially blessed that afternoon to have called her. She was indeed an integral part of my spiritual journey.

Later that night, I told Joe what I was going to do.

His reaction was positive.

"Whatever works for you."

"It is mind over matter," I said.

The next morning as I waited for my cab to take me to the airport, Joe called to wish me a safe journey.

We chatted for a moment, and then he asked, "Do you have Tatianna with you?"

For an instant, I was stunned to hear her name, and I thought he had meant to say Katarina. Then I realized he had taken me seriously the evening before!

I immediately felt a sense of lightness about me.

"Yes, she's right here, draped over my left shoulder, and we are going to have a wonderful journey together. I bet you think I have gone bonkers."

"It's not the way I would be, but if it works for you, then go for it."

"So you are not going to send the little men in the white coats to take me away?"

"Absolutely not."

As the airplane ascended, I ceremoniously reached across to my left shoulder with my right hand to where Tatianna was draped. I rubbed Tatianna's front paws—much like she used to knead my feet with her paws.

"Is it not ironic?—Now we are switching roles! We are off on an adventure. Please help keep me safe and enjoy the view," I said silently.

The rest of my trip to Midland went smoothly, and I had a restful night prior to the meeting.

As I waited for the meeting to start, I called upon Tatianna's spirit.

"Please help give me the strength to present to my thirty-five colleagues. Having you draped over my shoulder is a comforting feeling."

As I heard my name announced to come to the podium, I repeated rubbing Tatianna's paws as I had done on the airplane. Of course, no one else in the room knew what I had done. I successfully presented a new course concept and was deeply grateful for all the help that day.

In the stillness of the night following my Thursday afternoon presentation, I spoke to Tatianna.

"Thank you, my beloved Tatianna, for accompanying me on this illuminating journey. I realized today our bond has not been broken—it is continuous. Although invisible to others, it is highly visible to us. Our relationship has evolved to another dimension. I understand how much a part of my heart and soul you are. You have made a profound impact on my life. Our fifteen-and-one-half year journey together did not end on April 14; it has simply and dramatically changed. It is true that our physical journey has ended, because you are now a spiritual being. However, you are still at my side—here to help me, guide me, and love me unconditionally. You are still here to teach me more of life's lessons. I pray for the awareness to find the blessed lessons and messages hidden in my excruciating sorrow and loss. Although I long to look into your joyful blue eyes, feel the warmth of your soft fur, and hear the sound of your contented purr, all I have to do is have faith that all is as it should be at this moment in time. That is truly not an easy lesson to learn.

"I love you, Tatianna, always and forever. Someday, I will see you on the Rainbow Bridge, and it will be a glorious reunion!"

Home at Last
Tatianna and Linda

CHAPTER NINETEEN
TATIANNA'S ASHES

**A brief parting from those dear
is the worst man has to fear.**[1]
—W. B. Yeats

I arrived at the Palm Beach International Airport at noon on Saturday. It felt good to be back home. While I was waiting at baggage claim, I observed a man surprise his wife with a big welcome from their adorable dog. The dog was so excited and started barking and licking the woman. It brought tears to my eyes to witness this happy reunion. It reminded me of how reunions must be on the Rainbow Bridge.

In four hours, I would be retrieving Katie from the boarding kennel. Bob always fed the animals at 4:00 PM on the weekends, after the business had closed. Over the years, I had been allowed to get Tatianna and Katarina after business hours, depending on my travel schedule. I appreciated the extra time we got to spend together before the start of the workweek. Otherwise, if I arrived home after noon on Saturday, I would have had to wait until Monday morning to be reunited with my pals.

I took a cab home. I distinctly noticed that unlocking and opening the door did not stir tearful thoughts as it had before, although I was fully aware that Tatianna and Katarina were not waiting for me. At 3:40 PM, I left to go to the clinic in the hopes that Bob would be there early. He was outside, walking a basset hound. We went inside.

"Do you want to take Tattie's ashes?"

"Yes," I managed to utter.

The ashes had not been there on Tuesday when I had dropped off Katie. I had been dreading this moment. He departed to get the ashes, and I remained in the back hallway. I prayed that I could accept the box of ashes graciously and not become hysterical. Bob returned with a small wooden box. A piece of paper with a number on it was taped to the box. I figured that signified her place among all of the private cremations. I thanked Bob, and then we went to the upstairs kennel to get Katie. Katie was lying in her blue kennel case without its door in the cage. Bob lifted the case and Katie out and snapped the wire door onto it. I could not wait to get home to give her a proper welcome. I gathered up her extra food in one hand and held Tattie's ashes in the other. Bob carried Katie downstairs and set her in the front seat of my car. As I got into the driver seat, Katie was beside herself. She was pushing against the kennel door and reaching out with her paws. I put my fingers through the door, touched her, and tried to calm her down. Her welcome was touching.

"Oh, dear sweet Katie, please calm down. I am here with you now. You must have thought everyone had deserted you. But I will always take care of you. I love you so much. We will be safely home in six or seven minutes."

I drove out of the parking lot with rambunctious Katie in her kennel and Tatianna's remains in a small wooden box on the front seat. This was another first for me. Over the years, Tatianna had always ridden in the front seat, where I could touch her through the wire grate, and Katarina had taken the middle of the backseat, where I could stretch my fingers out to play with her. It had always been a jubilant homecoming for the three of us. But that afternoon was different and extremely difficult. I began sobbing uncontrollably. Poignant memories of Tatianna flooded my mind; one impression after the other bombarded me. I was literally reliving her life with us in quick flashes. I could not see the road or Katarina. Tatianna had been my delightful companion for almost sixteen years. Inevitably when I worked a long day and she had spent the day alone with Katarina, she immediately welcomed me when I returned. The same was true when I returned from vacations. If she had been fed late, she quickly forgave me. It did not matter if I was grieving, depressed, or distraught—her love was there to sustain me. I could be disheveled, and she still crawled into my lap. My hair could be a mess and my face a fright, and she still nuzzled me. I did not have to be perfect every moment for her to love me.

During our time together, she saw me through many poignant and significant adult experiences. She was there during the exit of my devoted orange marmalade cat, Noelle. She was with me during the quick entrance and exit of darling little Taittinger and for the arrival of her inseparable companion, Katarina. She was at my side during the entrance and tragic, untimely exit of my soul mate, Ken. She saw me through the sale of my longtime successful pet care business as well as the sudden exit of my father at Christmastime. She watched the entrance and exit of Marnie and saw me through the start of a second business and career. She stood by me during my new relationship with Joe. People came and went in my circle of life; pets came and went as well. Tatianna's resilience withstood that and more. Her longevity, influence, and impact in my life were profound.

As the stoplight changed, my tears subsided slightly, and I moved the car forward slowly. Katie continued to roll around in her kennel, and I realized she was beating her head on the door. I was afraid she was going to hurt herself. All I wanted to do was get the two of us home safely. I prayed to God to help me through this dreadful moment and to take care of us for the short drive.

Then I quieted down, and we made it home safely. I was very tired and went straight to bed. As I rested in bed with Katarina next to me, I reflected on all that had happened over the past few days. It became clear to me that there was a reason why Tatianna's ashes had not been ready on Tuesday when I dropped Katie off. For me to understand this particular lesson, I had to come home with Katie *and* Tattie, one in physical form on the seat next to me and one in the spiritual form draped over my shoulder. Tatianna's love was with us, guiding us safely home. I learned not to be afraid the next time I boarded Katie and brought her home alone. Tatianna would be with us, safely tucked away in our hearts, and she would have a grand view from my shoulder. She had become—without a doubt—one of God's little angel kitties.

What I had learned on my journey was that Tatianna was neither here nor there; she just *was*. She was wherever I was, just as she was always in my heart. So when I unlocked the door to the empty house earlier in the afternoon before picking up Katie, Tatianna was symbolically draped over my left shoulder.

I patted where I felt her paws would have been and said aloud, "Thanks, Tatianna, for helping us to get home safely."

EPILOGUE

**Dreams are illustrations
from the book your soul is writing about you.
—Marsha Norman**[1]

On Saturday, May 12, five weeks after Tatianna's passing, I awoke at 6:30 AM. I got up and manually turned on the sprinklers, which had been malfunctioning since Tatianna's last morning with me. I also fed Katie and went back to bed. She took two bites and immediately followed me. She was not accustomed to being fed that early any more than I was used to getting up that early. She snuggled close to me. My mind whirled with detailed thoughts of Tatianna's last month. The sadness overcame me, and I began to cry. I pulled the covers over my head. Katarina crawled under the covers and started licking away my tears. As we lay there, I heard a creaking noise from the hardwood floorboards near the dresser. My first and only inclination that particular morning was that Tatianna was there even though Katarina was nestled in bed with me at the moment. However, I had forgotten that Tatianna was no longer with us. I did not uncover my head to investigate. I fell asleep.

Later a very loud continuous scratching in the litter box—the kind Tatianna always exhibited—awoke me. I knew it was not Katarina, because she always jumped in and out of the litter box very quickly. I rolled over in bed, uncovered my head, and peered into the bathroom from the bed. There I saw a gray cat with her back to me. I could not believe what I was seeing. I thought, "Any minute now my eyes will adjust and I will see Katie." But the view became more definitive—it was Tatianna! She turned around in the box, and our eyes met. There was no mistaking those light-spilling blue eyes. She ran under the bed like she was scared or caught being disobedient, which she never did after being in the litter box. I got out of bed and reached underneath the bed. I touched her. I grabbed onto her and pulled her out.

"You are back," I said.

I held her ever so tightly and kissed her, feeling her warmth. I was astounded at how she looked. Her eye coloring was bright, clear, and beautiful. She had that full-of-life look about her, a vitality and alertness. She felt solid, and her coat was sleek and shiny. I still thought I was dreaming but realized it was her. I thought, "I cannot wait to tell people that Tatianna is back!" I wanted to go find Katie, who was not in the bedroom at the moment, and reunite her with Tatianna.

Then we were transported to this unfamiliar expansive building with a lobby and corridors going off all of the sides. There was a lot of hustle and bustle all around us. I met two of my university students there. One brought me a work life portfolio to be considered for college credit, and we had a lengthy, detailed conversation about the evaluation process of it. The other student brought me a bag of beautifully handcrafted pillows, and we talked about my antiques shop. I also saw my sister and brother-in-law, who were shopping in a huge fabric store. They were packaging a big box to mail home. I watched them do it, but I did not talk to them. At the other end of the building was Dr. Wright's office. I could not wait to show her Tatianna. This was indeed a miracle!

Tatianna was on my shoulder, and we were happily walking around the building. Then all at once, I sensed a lightness on my shoulder, and she was not there.

I started wailing, "Tatianna! Tatianna! Tatianna!"

I knew then it was a dream, and I would wake up at any second. I began frantically looking around the lobby for her, and I caught a glimpse of her. When our eyes met, she took off again, running down a long never-ending corridor. She was moving fast and low to the ground—almost crawling. She looked so healthy and well nourished, but her paws were yellowish, not the snow white that she had had. I wondered, "Why? Where has she traveled? Is she startled by the sounds?" Suddenly, Katie appeared and joined me in pursuit. We caught her. I was so relieved.

When I picked Tatianna up in my arms, we were back in my bed, and she was writing in a fast scrawl. I made out the name "Nikki," and she was drawing something with red, white, and blue colors that had a patriotic theme to it. But as the writing became faster and faster, I could not read it. The words literally flew onto the page. I thought, "This is not your writing, Tatianna, but it does remind me of my friend's writing." I was so confused. Then Tatianna signed the work "Steve," my brother's name, and I was even more perplexed because it was not Steve's handwriting.

At that moment, I woke up and realized the whole thing was a dream travel—or was it? I was absolutely drained. It was 9:00 AM, and almost three hours had passed. The dream had been so vivid in detail and color, and I rarely dreamed in color. I was trying to make some sense of it. "What had just happened? Is Tatianna telling me, 'I am here with you—I am healthy and whole and vibrant again, so do not worry about me'?" I had asked Tatianna before she died to please let me know she was okay or to get a message to me if she could. The night before this encounter, I had written in my journal that God's hands and Tatianna's paws were directing me to write this story. I wondered, "Is she telling me today, 'You have to do it and I will help you write it'? 'In fact, we will write our story together—just like in the dream where we are supporting one another and just like we always did in real life'? Has she really come back for a brief moment to see me?" But she knew this was not where she should be and knew she could not stay. That is why she ran under the bed and later ran quickly down the long corridor. She knew she could leave her spiritual realm for only a brief moment. She knew she needed to journey back to the Rainbow Bridge and wait for me. Was her mission to tell me to go on with my rich, earthly life that included Joe, Katarina, my students, my friends like Nikki, my family, my antiques shop, and my writing? Was she telling me to celebrate holidays as I always loved to do? Was she telling me to decorate my Christmas trees every year and to continue the cat ornament collection? Was she telling me to travel far and wide? Was she telling me that I would love and protect many more furry felines in my lifetime? Was she telling me that I would indeed go on after her, just like I had done after losing Noelle, Taittinger, Ken, my father, and Marnie? Was she telling me I would always have the courage and competitive spirit to reinvent my life whenever necessary? Was she telling me that on earth, time moves so fast and not to waste precious time by *not* pursuing my passions? Was she telling me I needed to get our extraordinary message out to the world?

I went to the kitchen to make a cup of tea and to record this incredible adventure in my journal. As I lifted my right hand up to open the cupboard, I could truly smell the essence of Tatianna on my forearm. Warm tears started streaming down my face. I knew in my heart that Tatianna had succeeded in getting a message to me—a message she knew I was now ready to decipher.

I recalled long ago how her extraordinary eyes drew me into her soul when I first brought her home. I always wondered what mysteries were hidden behind those miraculous blue eyes that pulled me to her like magnets. Intuitively, I knew those eyes, which snapped and sparked throughout her life, reflected important secrets. That day, I clearly understood one secret message when she returned to me and illuminated the windows to her soul. "Yes, I will write our book with your help. Thanks to you, Tatianna, I now know it is the purpose of my life. What a teacher you are!"

As I slowly lowered the teacup from the cupboard, I softly said, "I love you, Tatianna, always and forever. Someday I will see you on the Rainbow Bridge, and it will be a glorious reunion."

NOTES

Preface

1. Silvia Browne and Nancy Dufresne, *A Journal of Love and Healing* (Carlsbad, CA: Hayhouse, Inc., 2001), 8

Chapter One: Tatianna's Arrival

1. Irving Townsend, *Separate Lifetimes* (Exeter, NH: J.N. Townsend Publishing, 1986), 172

Chapter Two: Tatianna's First Year

1. Theophile Gautier, *My Household of Pets* (Boston: Roberts Brothers, 1882), 32–33

Chapter Three: Tatianna's New Friend, Taittinger

1. Robert Frederick, ed., *The Book of Cats: A Collection of Poetry and Prose in Celebration of Cats* (Bath, England: Robert Frederick Ltd., 1997), 9

Chapter Four: Tatianna and Katarina—A Love to Remember

1. Thomas Wolfe, *Look Homeward, Angel* (New York: Charles Scribner's Sons, 1929), 192

Chapter Five: Tatianna's Favorite Spots

1. Jane Austen, *Emma* (New York: Barnes & Noble Classics, 2004), 246

Chapter Six: Tatianna's Outdoor Escape

1. Laura Ingalls Wilder, 1. Laura Ingalls Wilder, http://www.oswego.edu/~dutton/csc366?quote/quotes.html

Chapter Seven: Tatianna's Unwelcome Sunday Visitor

1. Anne Morrow Lindbergh, *Gift From the Sea* (New York: Pantheon Books, 1955), 97

Chapter Eight: Tatianna's Relationship with Linda

1. Gunther Stuhlmann, ed., *The Diary of Anaïs Nin, Volume II, 1934-1939* (San Diego: Harcourt Brace & Company, 1970), 193

Chapter Nine: Tatianna and the Thanksgiving Guest

1. Irving Townsend, *Separate Lifetimes* (Exeter, NH: J.N. Townsend Publishing, 1986), 156

Chapter Ten: Tatianna Gets Ill

1. *Hannah Senesh: Her Life and Diary* (Woodstock, VT: Jewish Lights Publishing, 2004), 162

Chapter Eleven: Tatianna's Acupuncture Visit

1. George Eliot, *Middlemarch* (New York: Barnes & Noble Classics, 2003), 698
2. Cheryl Schwartz, DVM, *Four Paws Five Directions: A Guide to Chinese Medicine for Cats and Dogs* (Berkeley: Celestial Arts Publishing, 1996)

Chapter Twelve: Tatianna's Daily Ritual

1. Willa Cather, *Death Comes for the Archbishop* (New York: Vintage Books, 1990), 50

Chapter Thirteen: Tatianna's Triumphal Battle

1. Ted Mann Family Resource Center, Mary Jean Iron, *Normal Day*, http://www.cancerresources.mednet.ucla.edu/5_info/5d_archive_living/2001/normal_day.htm

Chapter Fourteen: Tatianna and the Christmas Cat Tree

1. Emily Dickinson, *The Collected Poems of Emily Dickinson* (New York: Barnes & Noble Books, 1993), 130

Chapter Fifteen: Tatianna's Triumphal Battle Winds Down

1. Louisa Mae Alcott, *Little Women* (New York: Children's Classics, 1987), 329

Chapter Sixteen: Tatianna's Last Morning

1. C.S. Lewis, *A Grief Observed* (San Francisco: Harper, 1961), 47
2. Laurel E. Hunt, ed., *Angel Whiskers: Reflections on Loving and Losing a Feline Companion* (New York: Hyperion), 35–36

Chapter Seventeen: The Hours After

1. Eleanor Roosevelt, *You Learn by Living: Eleven Keys for a More Fulfilling Life* (Louisville: Westminster John Knox Press, 1983), 29–30

Chapter Eighteen: Tatianna's Journey with Linda

1. Emily Dickinson, *The Collected Poems of Emily Dickinson* (New York: Barnes & Noble Books, 1993), 242

Chapter Nineteen: Tatianna's Ashes

1. Richard J. Finneran, ed., *The Collected Poems of W.B. Yeats* (New York: Scribner Paperback Poetry, 1996), 325

Epilogue

1. Sarah Ban Breathnach, *Simple Abundance: A Daybook of Comfort and Joy* (New York: Time Warner), 11-29

ABOUT THE AUTHOR

Linda A. Mohr is an educator, entrepreneur, and eternal animal lover. For more than thirty years, she has shared her life with feline companions, notably Tatianna, Noelle, Taittinger, Marnie, and Katarina. The experiences of living with and loving these precious pets—and learning to tell them good-bye—has given Linda tremendous insight into the mysterious, often miraculous, human-animal connection.

As owner of Pet Apothecary from 1977 to 1989, Linda pioneered the first pet business in Palm Beach County that offered evening hours and one-stop shopping for medical, boarding, supply, and grooming services. Through running this business, Linda often witnessed how an owner's love and devotion can help a beloved animal overcome seemingly insurmountable medical odds.

A professor at Northwood University's West Palm Beach campus, Linda received the Outstanding Faculty Award for five consecutive years and was honored in *Who's Who Among America's Teachers* in 2002 and 2003. She teaches marketing and management courses. She has a master's of business administration from Nova University, a master's of science from Purdue University, and a bachelor's of science from the University of Missouri.

Linda resides in Florida with her current feline friend Lexie Lee, a stray she adopted after Hurricane Jeanne in 2005. She continues to feel Tatianna's wise, loving presence at work in her life.

Linda encourages you to contact her at http://www.lindamohr.net with your remarks and reactions to *Tatianna*. Perhaps you would like to share your experience with a feline friend who had kidney disease. She would love to hear your heartfelt stories.

978-0-595-42677-5
0-595-42677-8

Printed in the United States
96038LV00002B/502-678/A

9 780595 426775